MIRACLE
PEOPLE
POWER

OTHER BOOKS BY THE AUTHOR

Doctor Van Fleet's Amazing New "Non-Glue Food" Diet

Guide to Managing People

How to Put Yourself Across with People

How to Use the Dynamics of Motivation

Power with People

The 22 Biggest Mistakes Managers Make and How to Correct Them

James K. Van Fleet

Miracle People Power

Parker Publishing Company, Inc.
West Nyack, N.Y.

Library of Congress Cataloging in Publication Data

Van Fleet, James K
  Miracle people power.

    1. Control (Psychology) 2. Success.
I. Title.
BF632.5.V36   158'.1   74-32439
ISBN 0-13-585497-0

This book is dedicated to my 3 children, whom I also consider to be my good friends—

Teresa Lynne Van Fleet Spain
Lawrence Lee Van Fleet
Robert James Van Fleet

What This Book Will Do for You

If there is one thing I have learned over the years from working with people, it is that people don't only want to get along with other people—*they want to dominate them*.

However, most persons make the basic mistake of trying to gain power with people by using force. They will always fail. Only slaves or prisoners can be dominated by force, and they will rebel at the first opportunity. Power with people by force cannot be long maintained.

If you're going to achieve lasting power with people, and if you're going to influence, control, and dominate them, you will have to use more sophisticated methods than force.

This book will give you those methods you can use to gain such power. In fact, the techniques you'll learn here are so subtle, yet so powerful, I've seen fit to call this book, MIRACLE PEOPLE POWER, for when properly used, each step will literally work a miracle for you with other people. You'll soon find that you won't have to use naked force or threats to get what you want. Instead, you'll get what you want because people will gladly do what you want them to do.

Here's exactly what these steps will do for you. Specifically, they will show you—

5

How to discover a person's innermost needs and desires
How to influence and control everyone you meet
How to conquer fear in yourself and others
How to know when, where, and on whom to use your power
How to get instantaneous results with people
How to get your own way every time
How to double and triple your power with the words you use
How to put miracle people power into everything you say
How to write letters that are loaded with miracle people power
How to control the actions and attitudes of complete strangers
How to overcome people's anger and bitterness, suspicion and
    mistrust
How to inspire the complete confidence of everyone in you
How to get people to cooperate and support you 110 percent
How to get the best of every argument
How to use a power play that never fails
How to issue orders that always get miraculous results
How to make others actually welcome your criticism
How to get others to do their best for you
How to handle problem people
How to fill your home life with excitement, joy, and happiness
How to keep your miracle people power at a high level all your
    life

When you put these techniques to work for yourself, you'll gain
miracle power with people. I know you will, for I've seen it happen
time after time with people just like those you'll meet on nearly
every page of this book.

So if you're ready now, let's get on with it, shall we?

James K. Van Fleet

Contents

Techniques You Can Use to Gain These 3 Benefits   207
How to Choose the Kind of Home Life You Want · How to Keep Your Marriage Fresh and Alive · How to Give Thanks and Honest Appreciation to Your Wife · Here's One of the Real Secrets to Joy and Happiness in Your Home · How to Be an Exceptional Sexual Partner · How to Work and Play Together · How to Enjoy Your Children

1

How Miracle People Power Reveals the Innermost Secret Needs and Desires of Others

Miracle people power is dependent upon your observing and understanding the secrets of human nature. As you grow in the skill and ability to do this, as you learn to look for what people think rather than say, you will develop this power.

Your first step in utilizing miracle people power, then, is to get inside people's minds so you can discover what they really want. You must find out what their innermost secret needs and desires are. When you do this, you will be able to understand what actually makes another person tick—what motivates him—what really turns him on. You'll know why he does the things that he does.

In this first chapter, then, you'll gain some fundamental knowledge about people and their basic needs and desires. In the remaining chapters, you'll discover the various techniques that will show you how to put this valuable information about people to work for yourself in any given situation. When you get your miracle people power up to its peak performance, you'll soon find that people will actually *want* to do what you want them to do.

Now you don't need to be a psychiatrist or a psychologist, nor do you need any sort of an advanced degree to be able to understand human nature so that you can discover the innermost secret needs and desires of other people.

The techniques you'll learn, not only in this chapter, but also in the rest of this book, are easy to understand, simple to use, and most important of all, they'll do the job for you. They'll unlock the door to your understanding of the deepest facets of human nature. These techniques will reveal what another person really wants . . . what his innermost, deepest, secret needs and desires actually are. Let me give you a quick for instance so you can see exactly what I mean.

How Allen White Read His Foreman's Mind

The other day I got a letter from Allen White, a young production supervisor with Western Electric. Here's what he said:

"Until I heard your talk, *How to Use the Dynamics of Motivation,*[1] about how to get people to want to do what you want them to do, I never knew about the innermost needs and desires the average individual has, nor did I understand the deep basic motives that move a person to do as he does.

"I'd been trying to sell my foreman on a change in work methods for some time, but I'd never been able to get my point across to him because I'd been emphasizing how much it would help me and my section. So I decided to try your ideas. First off, I analyzed the basic needs and desires you said every person has so I could find out which ones were most applicable to my boss. I came up with a need for a feeling of importance and recognition of efforts.

"So I approached him this way: 'Sam,' I said, 'if you could increase production by 10 percent and cut costs in the department at the same time, that'd make you look real good in the front office, wouldn't it?'

" 'It sure would,' he said. 'What do you have in mind, Allen?'

"I knew immediately I'd registered with him so I told him my plan. I made my entire pitch in terms of how he would benefit by my new procedure. He bought my proposal at once. And all because I'd learned to think and talk about what he wanted instead of what I wanted. Of

---

[1] Also a book. James K. Van Fleet, *How to Use the Dynamics of Motivation.* (West Nyack, New York: Parker Publishing Company, Inc., 1967).

course, *when I showed him how to get what he wanted, then I got what I wanted, too.*"

You'll also discover, just as Allen did, that when you make an honest effort to understand human nature, you'll be able to serve people better by helping them fulfill their innermost needs and desires. And in so doing, you'll automatically help yourself, too.

In fact, when you really know what a person's innermost needs and desires are, and when you do everything you can to help him fulfill those needs and desires,

YOU'LL GAIN THESE BENEFITS

You'll Have Power with People that Works Like Magic

When you know and understand the innermost needs and desires that motivate people to do what they do, when you make every effort to help them fulfill those needs and desires, you'll gain miracle power with people that seems to work just like magic for you.

You'll Save Time and Energy

When you know what a person really wants, you'll save a tremendous amount of time and energy. You won't have to go on a "fishing expedition." You can tailor your approach to fit his exact needs and concentrate your attention on that one specific point.

You'll Be Able to Influence and Control Everyone You Meet

As you study people to perfect your understanding of human nature, as you learn why people do the things they do and why they act the way they do, and as you learn to analyze their words and their actions to determine their innermost needs and desires, you'll find that your ability to influence and control every person with whom you come in contact continues to improve. Your success will be inevitable; you'll truly gain miracle power with people.

TECHNIQUES YOU CAN USE TO GAIN THE BENEFITS

How to Find Out Everything You Can About Your Subject

To achieve miracle power with people, you need useful information about them. You'll want to know a person's dominant desires for these are his most vulnerable areas—his major points of weakness. Then, just as Allen White did, you can use these dominant needs and desires to get what you want. Here's one technique you can use to gain that power.

Keep a Little Black Book

"Knowing each one of my people individually is a must to me," says Barry Young, an Orlando, Florida, department store manager. "I want to know immediately when something is bothering one of my employees.

"Each person has his or her own personality traits. I have to know what they are if I'm to understand that individual. So I keep a small notebook in my desk with each employee's name listed in it.

"I can turn to a certain page and find his age, his wife's name, how many children he has, their names, his hobbies, a little bit about his background, educational level, and any other pertinent information I consider to be worth while.

"A lot of times I need information like this to start the person talking about his problem. I want him to know that I'm interested in him—not just in the company and in the store."

You can keep a little black book on specific people, too. The information you record will be dependent upon your relationship with each person. For starters, though, here are some ideas you can use:

1. What are his main objectives in life?
2. What are his primary interests and concerns?
3. What are his dominant needs and desires?
4. What personal accomplishments is he proud of?
5. What are his hobbies?
6. How does he get along with people?

7. How does he accept praise?
8. How does he react to criticism?
9. What are his personal characteristics?
10. What are his likes and dislikes?
11. What makes him angry?
12. What makes him laugh?

What the Little Black Book Is *Not* Used for

Before you get the wrong idea about how to use your little black book, let me tell you right here it is not used to catch another person in some embarrassing act or compromising situation. It is not used for petty blackmail. Don't interpret this technique to be the same as Big Brother used in *1984*.[2]

Your purpose in keeping a little black book on another person is to find out what that other person wants so you can help him get it. When you do that, you'll be able to get what you want at the same time.

How to Use a Person's Basic Needs and Desires as a Guide to Gather Your Data

The ordinary, average, normal person has certain basic instinctive needs and desires. These needs and desires are things he feels deeply that he must have if he is to be completely happy. Some of these needs are quite evident and obvious. Others are much more obscure, hidden, and subtle. However, if any one of them is not fulfilled, the person will be restless, uneasy, and deeply dissatisfied with life.

When you find out what a person's deepest needs and desires are, and then show him how to gain them, you can write your own ticket. You can't help but become successful, for nothing will ever be able to stop you.

---

[2] George Orwell, *1984* (New York, New York: Harcourt, Brace and Company, Inc., 1949).

The basic needs and desires the average normal person has are these:

1. Love in all its forms.
2. Financial success: money and the things money will buy.
3. Recognition of efforts; reassurance of worth.
4. Ego-gratification; a feeling of importance.
5. A sense of personal power.
6. A sense of roots; belonging somewhere.
7. The opportunity for creative expression.
8. New experiences.
9. Good health: freedom from sickness and disease.
10. Liberty and freedom.
11. A sense of self-respect, dignity, and self-esteem.
12. Emotional security.

I have not listed these basic needs and desires in any particular order of importance. The point is, a person cannot be completely happy if any single one of them is not fulfilled.

I think you will find, just as I have, that *whatever a person is lacking at the moment he has the greatest need and desire for.* Your job is to use your miracle people power to find out which specific need or desire is most important to the person at that time.

You should also remember that a person's needs and desires can and do change from time to time. What he needed yesterday may not be what he needs most of all today. That's why you'll need to keep your little black book up to date all the time.

HOW TO USE HIS BASIC DESIRES TO GET WHAT YOU WANT: THREE EXAMPLES

How to Profit from a Person's Desire for Love

Ken Gilbert sells Kenmore washing machines and dryers for Sears Roebuck. There are six salesmen in his department and Ken outsells every one of them. Here's his secret:

"Most salesmen use the four standard benefits of gain, safety, pride, and convenience to sell their product," Ken says. "However, they miss the boat completely by not using the most potent sales tool of all: *love*. Love is the psychological lever that will do the job when all those others fail.

"For instance, when I'm ready to close a sale and the man still hesitates, I say to him sincerely, *'Your wife will love you for buying it.'* That one sentence has sold more washers and dryers for me than anything else."

Recognizing a Person's Efforts Leads Him to Do His Best for You

All of us feel a deep need for appreciation of our work. For instance, if you want your children to do better in their school work and bring home good grades, then praise them. They need recognition of their efforts just as much as grownups do, if not more so. Tell them what a good job they've done. Or do as Sam Hastings does.

> "Whenever my son, Larry, or my daughter, Teresa, brings home a good grade card or wins an award of some sort in school, I show them how much I appreciate what they've done," Sam says. "We celebrate and make a festive occasion out of it. We take them out to dinner at their favorite restaurant and then on to a movie or a show afterward. Has it paid off? You bet it has. I haven't seen anything below a B from either one of them for over two years now."

You can do as Sam does or you can work up your own techniques to give your children recognition for their efforts. But whatever you do and however you do it, remember to tell them in words, too, how happy you are about what they've done. *"I am proud of you"* are five of the most powerful words you can ever use to let another person know how much you appreciate his efforts.

You can use these words any time, not only on your children, but also on your boy friend or girl friend, your husband or wife, your employees, associates, and friends. Those five little words will increase your miracle people power a hundredfold. When you use them, people will go all out to do as you want them to do.

Want a Favor from a Friend? Here's How:

> "I have a neighbor who's a real green thumb," says Ed Jennings. "I'm not, so whenever I need help, I turn to Stan. But I always word my request for a favor in such a way he can't refuse what I ask. I make

him feel important and superior to me by showing respect for his knowledge and his ability.

"I'll say, 'Stan, I need your expert advice on this. Will you give me your opinion? What would you do if you were in my place?' Well, whatever it is, it seems he always ends up doing it for me, whether it's pruning a tree, planting a shrub, fertilizing my lawn, or loaning me his power saw.

"Why, one time when I was having trouble with crabgrass and asked him what to do, he planted more than a hundred plugs of zoysia grass from his own seed bed and wouldn't take a cent in return."

So next time you need a favor from a friend, don't think only of yourself and what you can get out of him. Figure out what you can do for the other person instead. One thing you can always do is make him feel important and superior to you by showing respect for his knowledge and asking for his opinion.

How to Get a Person to Reveal His Innermost Desires to You

The easiest way to find out what a person really likes or wants is simple. *Ask him.* Don't be afraid to do so. You can get specific answers to your questions if you use the question words *who, what, when, where, why, how,* and *how much.* Here are a few examples:

> "*What* would you like to do on our next date, Mary?"
> "*Where* would you like to go for dinner tomorrow, Sally?"
> "Exactly *when* were you planning on doing it, Hank?"
> "Specifically *how* can I help you, George?"
> "Would you mind telling me *why* you don't want it, Sam?"

The continual use of question words over a period of time cannot help but bring a person's true feelings to the surface. It will take patience, ingenuity, and work on your part, but it will pay you tremendous dividends.

"Everybody wanted a date with the new secretary," says Tim Kelly. "I think every single guy in the office asked her to go out the first week she was here, but she just kept right on saying *no* to them.

"I wanted a date with Linda, too, but I didn't rush at her like that. I spent a couple of weeks asking her a few questions here and there and listening to her answers. I also took part in general conversations with her and the rest of the office help at coffee breaks and paid close attention to everything she said.

"Soon I knew a great deal about her and what her interests were. I found out she was an outdoors type. She liked swimming, tennis, golf, horseback riding, picnics in the woods, long drives in the country. She didn't care much for movies, dancing, and night life.

"When I asked her for our first date, I was specific about what we were going to do. I suggested a ride up the coast to a good beach where we could swim, walk in the sand, get a suntan, and then barbecue some steaks later on in the evening.

"She accepted my offer immediately. Why? Well, everyone else had just told her what *they* were going to do on their date. I was the first one who found out what *she* was interested in and what *she* liked to do."

How to Get the Real Truth from an Individual

Although question words will get the answer for you most of the time, another phrase that can be used most successfully to find the hidden motive behind what a person does or does not do is this:

"Is there any other reason?"

You see, a person almost always has two reasons for doing or not doing something: *one that sounds good and the real one.*

That's why you have to keep digging away to get a person to reveal his innermost thoughts to you. Once you know the *real reason* behind his actions, you can put your miracle people power to work so you can get him to do what you want him to do.

"I'd lost one of our company's best clients and my boss was really upset about it," Jack Miller says. "He told me to get that account back or else. So I went back to see the owner. I told him I had to know *why* we'd lost his business, or I was going to lose my job.

"He gave me a number of reasons, but I kept right on digging for more information for I wasn't fully satisfied with his answers. I just kept right on repeating, 'Yes sir, but *is there any other reason* you've stopped buying from us?'

"Finally he told me straight out that because of a particular incident that had taken place, he didn't trust me or my company. Well, this was a tough blow to take, but now that I had the real reason out in the open, at least I could tackle the problem and try to solve it.

"And things did work out that way for me. Now that I knew the real reason behind his actions, I was able to find out *why* he felt the way he did and *what* I had done to create that feeling. It took quite a while to get things straightened out, but he's doing business with us again, and that's what counts."

So you see, if you don't get the real reason for a person's actions at first, keep right on plugging. Just keep asking more questions until you do.

How You Can Draw a Person Out: Seven Fail-Safe Methods

Getting a person to talk about himself and what he wants out of life more than anything else is easy when you use these seven techniques:

1. Forget your own self-interests completely.
2. Be sincerely interested in the other person.
3. Pay close attention to everything he says and does.
4. Encourage him to talk about himself.
5. Always talk in terms of the other person's interests to find out what he really wants.
6. Practice patience.
7. Make the other person feel important—and do it sincerely.

Now that you know the 12 basic needs and desires the average normal person has, let's move right on to the next chapter so I can show you in more detail how you can use them to increase your miracle people power and influence and control everyone you meet.

2

How to Use Miracle People Power to Influence and Control Everyone You Meet

In Chapter 1 on miracle people power, I told you about the 12 basic needs and desires every person has. I also told you why it was so important to find out everything you could about an individual as well as some of the methods you could use to obtain that information. Please keep those basic concepts in mind throughout the remainder of this book for they form the foundation upon which all else is built.

With that in mind, then, let us turn our attention to the second chapter. I want to show you in more detail how to put that information you've gained about a person to work in any given situation. I want to get right down to specifics—the nuts and bolts of how you can use your miracle people power to influence and control everyone you meet. Here's a concrete example to show you exactly what I mean:

How to Use a Person's Most Vulnerable Point to Your Own Advantage

"A few years ago, I decided to sell our house in Springfield so I could buy one out in the country," Dave Andrews told me. "I called the Landmark Real Estate Company and they sent a salesman, Bill

Evans, out to see me. We talked for a while. Or I should say that I talked. Actually, Bill asked questions and I answered them.

" 'You have a beautiful home here, Dave,' he said. 'Good part of town, excellent location, conveniently close to a new shopping center. Why on earth do you want to sell it and buy another house?

" 'Is it too small for your needs? I understood you to say all your children were grown and gone. Or is it too large for you now? Does the room arrangement or space utilization dissatisfy you? Why don't you like your house, Dave? Tell me what's wrong with it so I'll be better able to know exactly how I can help you.'

" 'Bill, I'll tell you the straight truth,' I said. 'There's absolutely nothing wrong with our house. I like it a great deal. If I could just pick it up and move it somewhere else, I'd keep it.

" 'You see, when we first moved here, we had a beautiful view of the valley out the front room window: green fields and trees. Now all I can see is that new two-story house across the street. And the same thing is true in my back yard. All I can look at are my neighbor's garbage cans, his doghouse, the tool storage shed, and a barbecue pit. I want a home with a decent view I can enjoy.'

" 'Good. Now I know exactly what you want and I have just the place you're looking for, Dave,' Bill said. 'Twenty miles out south of town. A beautiful home built on top of a hill. You can see for miles around. It has a gorgeous breath-taking overlook of the James River valley from the front porch. Nothing but green trees and miles of rolling pasture land. You'll love it, Dave. It's just what you're looking for.'

"So we drove out to see the place. Bill was right. It was everything I wanted. But the price was high. 'You're asking too much, Bill,' I said. 'My house is a newer one and you know I can't begin to get that kind of a price for it.'

"Bill didn't argue. 'Could be, Dave,' he said. 'But just look at that view of the lake. No one'll ever be able to build anything that will keep you from seeing it. That view belongs to you from now on. No one will ever be able to take it away from you.'

" 'But I don't think I can afford it, Bill,' I said. 'I don't have that kind of money lying around loose, and besides . . .'

" 'Financing is no problem, Dave,' Bill said, interrupting me. 'I know of no less than five lending institutions who would loan you the money today without a single question. Your credit rating is tops. I checked that before I ever left the office.

" 'And just look at that view from the front room window here, Dave. Isn't that absolutely spectacular? No house across the street to block your view of the beautiful James River valley. And there never will be. The way the hill drops off, you don't need to worry about anyone ever building on it. This is exactly what you asked for, Dave. This is precisely what you said you wanted.'

"Each time I talked price or money or financing, Bill talked scenery and a beautiful view of the lake and the James River valley, for he knew full well that's what I was primarily interested in. I'd already told him that back at my house. By asking questions and by listening to my answers, Bill had found my main point of interest. He'd found my most vulnerable point and he concentrated on that.

"So I bought the house. Or I should say I bought the view, for that's what Bill actually sold me. He sold me the view and the scenery . . . the lake and the trees . . . the James River valley and its rolling pasture land. He just threw in the house as an extra bonus; it was an additional dividend.

"Now I'd never met Bill Evans before that day. He and I were complete strangers until I bought that house. But just as soon as Bill found out exactly what I wanted and then showed me how to get it, he took charge of the situation. He held me in the palm of his hand for he was in complete control."

You can use the same techniques Bill Evans used with Dave Andrews to get what you want, too. When you find out precisely what a person wants and then show him how to get it, when you discover a man's most vulnerable point and then concentrate on that, and on that alone, you'll be able to influence and control everyone you meet, too, whether they're a stranger or not. In fact, when you do that,

YOU'LL GAIN THESE BENEFITS

How You'll Be Able to Influence the Thoughts and Actions of a Total Stranger

The moment you find out exactly what a person wants and then show him how to get it, you'll be in complete command of the situation the same way Bill Evans was. You'll be able to influence the thoughts and ideas of a complete stranger. You'll have the ability to control the decisions and actions of a person you've never met before when you show him precisely how to get what he wants.

How Controlling His Decisions Will Help You

When you can influence and control another person's thoughts and actions, when you show him how he'll get what he wants if he does as you want him to do, you'll make more money and gain more of the material benefits of life for yourself. You can't help but become successful, for finding out what a person wants and showing him how to get it is the most important secret of business and salesmanship.

Knowledge that Means Unlimited Power for You

When you know what another person really wants and then show him how to get it, you'll have a miracle people power in your grasp that few persons understand and even fewer ever possess.

If you know everything there is to know about a person, you can use that knowledge for your own benefit and to your own advantage. When you know what your husband wants, what your boss is thinking, what your competitor is doing, what your girl friend has on her mind, what the teacher is planning—you're truly in a most enviable position.

Finding out specifically what people want and then helping them get it is not only the most important secret of business and salesmanship, but it is also the number one rule in all your relationships with other people. It is a real key to miracle people power and a definite sound philosophy to practice and live by.

TECHNIQUES YOU CAN USE TO GAIN THE BENEFITS

Although the techniques you need to influence and control everyone you meet are all right there in the example of how Bill Evans sold a house in the country to Dave Andrews, I want to break them down for you individually so you'll have a clear understanding of how you can use each one of them yourself.

The formula to power, influence, and control over other people is broken down into three simple techniques:

1. Know how you can fulfill one or more of a person's innermost needs and desires.
2. Find out *specifically* what a person wants.
3. Help him get what he wants.

When you look over these three techniques, you can see how Bill Evans used them. First of all, Bill knew what he had to offer. He knew how he could fulfill a person's innermost needs and desires. Second, he found out specifically what Dave was looking for. Third, Bill showed Dave exactly how he could get what he wanted.

Now let's look at those three techniques in even more detail so you can see how you can make them work for you, too.

Knowing How You Can Fulfill One or More of a Person's Innermost Needs and Desires

This technique requires two things of you. The first requirement is that you know and understand and appreciate the average normal person's innermost needs and desires. The second one is that you must know exactly how your product or your service or how you yourself can fulfill that person's basic needs and desires.

You already know what those innermost needs and desires are. Now you need to analyze your own product, service, or proposition to find out exactly how you can help your listener and which of his basic needs and desires you can fulfill. To do this, you need knowledge about what you have to offer. You must know exactly how you can help a person and what you can do for him.

Bill Evans knew how to do that when he sold Dave a house. He didn't just sell a house. He offered Dave liberty from the restrictions and crowded conditions of city living. He gave him the chance to escape from the congestion, the pollution, and the noise of traffic. He offered Dave the opportunity to live as he wanted to live and to enjoy the unspoiled beauty of nature. Dave also gained a sense of personal power over his environment when he knew no one would ever be able to spoil his view of the lake and the James River valley.

When Dave was able to fulfill these basic needs, he was also able to gain emotional security, for emotional security cannot be achieved unless you are able to fulfill all your innermost desires.

A good way to learn how big companies and corporations slant their advertising toward the fulfillment of your innermost needs and desires is to analyze their TV commercials and study their newspaper and magazine advertisements. It's a lot of fun and highly informative. You can learn a lot by watching how the professionals do it.

Finding Out *Specifically* What a Person Wants

After you know exactly what you have to offer, your next step is to find out *specifically* what a person wants. If you will remember, I told you back in Chapter 1 that *whatever a person is lacking at the moment he has the greatest need and desire for*. And that's your job: to discover his greatest need and desire; to find out exactly what he wants.

And what's the best way to find out? That's right; by asking questions. Asking questions is still the most reliable and fastest way to find out precisely what your listener wants.

In Chapter 1, you also saw that you can get specific answers to your questions when you use the question words *who, what, when, where, why, how,* and *how much.* Here I want to tell you about some of the benefits you can gain by asking questions and using those simple question words.

Questions Help Your Listener Concentrate His Attention. By asking questions you can help a person focus his attention where you want it. He literally sells himself on your idea and then talks himself into believing it was his own idea in the first place. When you ask questions, you help a person make up his mind about what he actually wants.

"I've found the lecture method to be the poorest way to teach," says Joyce Hopkins, a high school history teacher. "When I ask questions and give my students the chance to answer them fully, it helps them concentrate their attention on the subject matter at hand.

Their minds don't wander away; they stay more alert. Not only that, questions stimulate full group participation and discussion."

Questions Make a Person Feel Important. When you ask a person for his opinion or his idea on anything, you make him feel more important. This in itself fulfills one of his innermost needs and desires. When you show him that you respect his opinion on the subject, he'll be more likely to respect yours and do as you want him to do.

"Want to have a happy marriage?" says Dr. Gerald Beasley. "Then pay attention to your partner; make your spouse important. How? One of the easiest ways I know is to ask questions. Just be sure they're the right kind of questions—ones that are designed to make the person important, needed, and useful.

"For instance, if you're the wife, ask him questions to get him to talk about himself, his work, and so on. And if you're the husband, do the same thing. A wife often feels left out of major decisions. Ask for her opinion. Let her know that you value and respect her judgment."

You'll Keep from Talking Too Much. I've seen people lose an argument and salesmen lose a sale because they talk when they should be listening. When you ask questions, the other person has the chance to tell you what he thinks and what he wants. All you need do is keep quiet and give him the opportunity to talk.

Raymond Campbell is in charge of industrial relations for the Mono Manufacturing Company in Joplin, Missouri. "Most people think my job is solving employee problems or settling labor grievances," Ray says. "Actually, I let people solve their own problems by talking them out to me. I just act as a sounding board for their frustrations. I ask a few questions here and there to stimulate their thinking. Then I sit back and listen. Keeps me from talking too much and spoiling things."

You Can Avoid Getting into an Argument. By asking questions, you can find out what the other person's idea is first. If you tell him what you think, if you give him your opinion first, you expose your own position. You may suddenly find yourself at odds with him

and lose all possibilities of getting your own way. If you don't agree
with what he says, don't tell him so point-blank. Use Jerry Dunlap's
method to change his method.

"I don't tell a person straight out I don't agree with him," Jerry
says. "Instead, I say, *'Don't you think* it might work better this way,
George?' *'Don't you feel* this would save you more time, Anna?'
'Doesn't this seem like a good way to do it, Mary?'

"This way I'm telling a person in a courteous way what I think
and I'm asking him at the same time to respond with his opinion or
idea. It gets much better results than saying, 'Do it this way, period!' "

**When You Ask Questions, You Can Find Out Specifically What
a Person Wants.** A question is still the quickest way to find out what
another person really wants. Questions help you find the key issue,
a person's most vulnerable point, his major weakness, his greatest
desire.

When you do discover his main point of interest or his most
important need—concentrate on that and on that alone. Don't
ramble around aimlessly from point to point scattering your fire.
You can use this one key issue to get your own way.

Helping Him Get What He Wants

After you find out specifically what a person wants, then you must
help him get it. Take Bill Evans again, for instance. Just to find out
what Dave wanted was not enough. Bill had to help Dave get what
he wanted the easiest way possible.

Bill did this by finding out that Dave's credit rating was okay . . .
that several lending institutions would lend him the money . . . by
showing him that he really could afford to buy the house. Bill did
everything he could to help Dave get what he wanted. And he did it
in such a way that Dave had no choice but to say yes. That's what
you must do for your listener, too.

Now let me give you another example here so you can see how
this technique will work in every kind of situation.

"A few years ago when I was a general foreman for the St. Louis plant, one of our Canadian plants ran into all sorts of production problems," Hugh Curtis says. "The vice president in charge of manufacturing up in Dayton told our plant manager, Glen Dawson, to transfer someone up there to straighten things out. Glen told our production superintendent, Joe Freeman, that he could go or that he could send me. Well, Joe picked me to go.

"It couldn't have been a worse time for me to move. My youngest son was graduating from college; my wife had just come home from the hospital; my oldest daughter's baby was due in June; we were right in the middle of building a new house.

"I wanted to stay where I was in the worst way, but I didn't want to give Joe a lot of excuses for not wanting the transfer either. I gave a lot of thought about how to handle it. Here's what I finally told him:

" 'Joe, you know I'm really honored by your picking me to go up to Canada to help them out,' I said, 'but I just wonder how they'll react to a general foreman telling a plant manager where he's wrong.

" 'Now if you were to go, there'd be no problem like that. After all, you're the production superintendent here and you act in the plant manager's place when Glen is gone. They'd listen to you.

" 'Not only that, it would really make you look good up in Dayton when you straighten up their mess. I really think an important job like that needs a big man like you with your experience and know-how to solve their problems, Joe.'

"Well, Joe took the job. You see, I was able to show him how he could fulfill several of his basic needs and desires by taking this transfer. Specifically he acquired: a feeling of importance; recognition of efforts; a sense of personal power; further financial success in the form of a promotion. These were Joe's most vulnerable points.

"But if I'd approached Joe with all the reasons why I didn't want to go, I'd be there and he'd still be here."

Now at first glance, you might think that to use a person's most vulnerable points to your own advantage has a sinister sound to it. Nothing of the sort. There's nothing evil about the idea at all. You're actually using a person's most vulnerable points to help him get what he wants.

You see, the only way you can ever find out what a person really wants is to discover the main issue—this will be his most vulnerable point—and then concentrate on that and on that alone.

Only then will you be able to help a person by showing him how to get what he really wants. And when you help another person get what he wants, you automatically get what you want, too.

Sometimes a person isn't really sure of what he wants most. He has to be shown what he wants just as Hugh Curtis showed Joe Freeman. So if a person isn't sure, help him find out. That's part of your job, too.

3

How to Conquer Fear with
Miracle People Power

In Chapter 3, you'll see that you can take a big stride toward increasing your miracle people power when you show people how to overcome their fears. People are always looking for information that will free them from their worries and their anxieties. If you want to be successful in dealing with people, then give them that information they want and need so much. This idea has an extremely practical application as you'll see right now:

How Art Ingle Helps People Overcome Their Fears

Art Ingle is a driving instructor in Los Angeles for the Safeway Automobile Driver's Training School. Art says one of the major aspects of his job is showing people how to overcome their fear of driving a car and how to gain confidence in themselves and in their own abilities.

"I constantly reassure my students and tell them there is absolutely no reason whatever why they cannot learn how to be a safe and dependable driver," Art says.

"One of the things our office does to help us is to find out as much as possible about the person first, including the hobbies or special skills that he has. I can then use this information to show the person

that if he was able to succeed in accomplishing some difficult achieve-
ment, then learning to drive a car is no harder and that he has absolutely nothing to be afraid of.

"For instance, suppose the individual can play golf, bowl, swim,
play tennis, ride a bicycle, play a guitar, cook a meal, or whatever.
I point out to that person that he or she wasn't born knowing how to
do all these things. The fact that he learned how to do them means
that he is intelligent and capable and that he can also learn to drive
a car.

"It doesn't matter at all what the person has learned to do well. I
use that accomplishment to overcome his fear of driving a car and to
instill confidence in himself even before he gets behind the wheel."

Most People Have One or More of These Fears

First of all, let me say you can't show others how to conquer their
fears unless you're free from fear yourself. All the techniques you'll
learn in this chapter, then, have a dual function: you can use them
to get rid of your own fears; you can also use them to show others
how to get rid of their fears. In both instances, you will be able to
expand your miracle people power.

*A primary motivator for most people is self-centered fear—the
fear that they might lose something they already possess, or the fear
they will fail to gain something they are trying to attain.*

Almost every one of us, at one time or another in life, suffers with
one or more of these eleven basic fears:

1. Fear of failure.
2. Fear of criticism.
3. Fear of making a decision.
4. Fear of not being important.
5. Fear of poverty.
6. Fear of loneliness or loss of someone's love.
7. Fear of loss of liberty.
8. Fear of sickness and ill-health.
9. Fear of old age.
10. Fear of death.
11. Fear of the unknown.

Now as I've already said, almost everyone will suffer from one or more of these basic fears at some time in life. As you learn how to conquer your own fears by using the techniques I'll give you here, your miracle people power will automatically develop and expand. You'll have much more confidence in yourself and in your own abilities. And as your own self-assurance increases, you'll develop even greater confidence in dealing with other people and showing them how to overcome their fears, too. When that happens,

YOU'LL GAIN THESE BENEFITS

1. People will trust you and have confidence in you.
2. They'll look to you for advice, help, and guidance.
3. People will follow your recommendations; they'll do as you want them to do.

TECHNIQUES YOU CAN USE TO GAIN THE BENEFITS

How to Interpret and Understand a Person's Motives

"Every human motive has both a positive aspect and a negative aspect," says Dr. Clifford Lawrence, a Chicago psychiatrist. "When an individual says or does something, he is striving to achieve a goal, a reward, or something he wants very much. At the same time, he is making an effort to separate himself as far as possible from that which he hates or fears.

"For instance, the average normal individual wants everyone to like him. His actions are therefore motivated by his desire for acceptance. Simultaneously, from the negative viewpoint, he is goaded by the fear of not being accepted by others.

"The man who hoards money is driven by an abnormal fear of poverty. The one who insists on being center-stage at all times is obsessed by the fear of not being important. The man who indulges constantly in extramarital affairs is filled with a compulsion to prove his masculinity.

"The greater the desire to win approval and acceptance from others, to hoard money, to be important, or to make love to many women— the greater the internal fear that drives the individual to do as he does."

How to Find Out What People Are Really Afraid of

Why is it so important to find out what people are really afraid of? Because it's a quick and easy way to find out what people want most of all. You see, you can easily determine in short order what people want by finding out what they are afraid of. What people want will always be the opposite of what they fear.

So when you find out what a person is afraid of, you'll know what he wants, and you can help him get it. As I told you in Chapter 2, finding out what a person wants and helping him get it is one of the best methods you can ever use to influence and control everyone you meet.

Now no one is going to come right out and tell you point blank what it is that he fears. You must ask leading questions and then listen attentively to what the other person says. Listen, not only to what he says, but also, to what he doesn't say. Learn to listen between the lines, too.

And watch for certain key words in the conversation. Such words as *fear, dread, afraid, uneasy, anxious, alarmed, worry, concern, scared,* and the like will serve as definite and tangible clues as to what a person is really afraid of or worried about.

Let a Person Know How You Can Free Him from His Fears

Let a person know at once that you can free him from his fears and his anxieties. A good way to do this is to use specific sentences in your conversation that will let him know how you can help him get rid of his worries and his concerns. Here are a few examples to help you get started:

> I can put your mind completely at ease on this.
> You'll never have to worry about that again.
> There's absolutely no reason for you to be afraid.
> You have nothing at all to fear.
> Don't be scared about that.

There's no reason for you to be concerned.
I understand your anxiety; I'll handle it for you.

How to Get Rid of Fear in Three Simple Steps

You can use these three steps to overcome your own fears or you can use them to show others how they can conquer theirs:

1. Admit your fear.
2. Analyze your fear to see if it's justified.
3. Take the necessary action to get rid of your fear.

Admit Your Fear

When you admit your fear, you've taken the first step toward solving your problem. Most people do not like to admit their fear for they think it is a confession of weakness. The exact opposite is true. Take an alcoholic, for example. When he admits that he's powerless over alcohol, as he does in the first step of the Alcoholics Anonymous program, he's on his way to recovery. The same thing happens when you admit your fear, too. You get it out in the open where you can pin it down and do something about it.

In his marvelous book, *How I Raised Myself from Failure to Success in Selling,*[1] Frank Bettger tells how he completely lost his nerve on his first big call on an important leader in the automobile industry, a Mr. Archie E. Hughes.

"As his secretary ushered me into his luxuriously furnished office I became increasingly nervous," Mr. Bettger says. "My voice trembled as I began to speak. Suddenly I lost my nerve completely and just couldn't go on. There I stood shaking with fear. Mr. Hughes looked up in astonishment. Then, without knowing it, I did a wise thing, a simple little thing that turned the interview from a ridiculous failure to success. I stammered, 'Mr. Hughes . . . I . . . uh . . . I've been trying to see you for a long while . . . and, uh . . . now that I'm here, I'm so nervous and scared I can't talk!'

---

[1] Frank Bettger, *How I Raised Myself from Failure to Success in Selling* (Englewood Cliffs, New Jersey: Prentice-Hall, Inc., 1949).

"Even while I spoke, to my surprise, my fear began to leave me. My dazed head quickly cleared, my hands and knees stopped shaking. Mr. Hughes suddenly seemed to become my friend. He obviously was pleased that I should regard him as such an important individual."

As Mr. Bettger goes on to say, this was an important turning point in his career. He found that by admitting his fear he was able to take the first step toward conquering it.

You can do the same if you'll remember this one simple rule:

WHEN YOU'RE AFRAID—ADMIT IT

Analyze Your Fear to See if It's Justified

Once you've admitted exactly what it is that you're afraid of, then you need to analyze your fear to see if it's truly justified. If it is, you can do something about solving it; if it isn't justified, you can stop worrying about it.

Let's talk first about unjustified or imaginary fear. Here's an example of what it can do to a person:

"I used to be afraid to speak up in a conference," Roger Nelson says. "I thought my ideas might sound stupid and people would laugh at me. I was afraid my thoughts weren't well enough organized to present at a meeting. And then I always felt someone else might have a better idea.

"But when I heard others offer the same idea I'd had and no one laughed, I realized that my fears weren't justified. They were entirely imaginary and self-generated. Now I speak up and say what I think without hesitation."

Now then. Let's talk about you. Is your fear because of something bad that's happened to you in the past? Have you had some unfortunate previous experience? We've all had them. They're over and done with; forget them. Very few people can cross the river of life without getting their feet wet. Or perhaps your fear is based on a false assumption just as Roger's was. Then find out the truth for yourself and get rid of your fear.

Maybe you're afraid of your boss as so many people are. Why

should you be? Are you afraid he's going to raise Cain with you for something you've done? Why? Have you really done something wrong? Are you afraid he's going to fire you? Why? Do you deserve to be fired? Has your work been sloppy and inefficient? Do you come to work late all the time? Have you been stealing from your boss? If your answer to all these questions is "no," then you have nothing at all to worry about. You're giving yourself stomach ulcers and cardiac flutter for no good reason whatever.

My advice is never to worry and fret about what you think other people might think about you. To do so is a complete waste of time.

What do you do if your fear is justified? For instance, if you're afraid you won't get promoted because you lack knowledge, then you should do the obvious thing: gain the proper knowledge.

Or if you're afraid your people might let you down, you can do as Steve Olson, a district sales manager for Mutual of Omaha, did.

"I was always afraid some of my branch salesmen would make some bad mistakes in handling some of our big accounts," Steve says. "Part of my fear was justified for serious mistakes were possible. So I decided to do everything I could to prevent errors and then stop worrying about it.

"First, I made sure all our sales people were well trained. Next, I made up a corrective plan of action just in case something did go wrong. Third, I realized that further worrying on my part about the problem was a complete waste of time and energy."

Steve is so right. If your fear is justified, do whatever you can do to eliminate your fear. Then stop worrying about it. You cannot control the whole world. A tornado, an earthquake, even a drunken driver can cause a tragedy in your life. You must simply learn to accept the things you cannot change.

Take the Necessary Action to Get Rid of Your Fear

The final step in conquering fear is to translate your analysis into the necessary action. And some kind of action is required for no action at all is usually more detrimental than too much activity.

If you're afraid and take no action whatever to control your fear, you will never be able to master it. For instance, the person who is afraid of everything—learning to swim, driving a car, getting married, buying a home, starting his own business—never will be able to overcome his fears of doing anything unless he does something positive about them. To conquer your fear, you must take definite concrete action of some kind. Here are two methods you can use to do just that:

1. Act as if it were impossible to fail.
2. Do the thing you fear to do.

Act as if It Were Impossible to Fail

If you'll notice, I have emphasized that you must *act* as if it were impossible to fail. I do not mean that you should not think about what you are going to do to defeat your fear; you should. But you must do much more than just think about it. I repeat, you must act. If you only think and do no more than that, you're just pretending—you're daydreaming. Instead of doing that, do as Lloyd Page does:

"I never worry about the possibility of failure," Lloyd says. "I have complete confidence in myself and my own abilities. I've found that a bad decision carried through with vigor and force has much more chance of succeeding than a good one that is carried out without drive and enthusiasm.

"Of course I still make mistakes. I wouldn't be human if I didn't. But I never give up. I'll never fail as long as I keep on trying. I will always succeed eventually as long as I act as if it were impossible to fail."

Do the Thing You Fear to Do

Do the thing you fear to do and you'll gain the power to do it. In 98 out of every hundred cases, this is the best solution you can use to get rid of your fear. You'll gain the necessary knowledge and experience that will help you get rid of your emotional insecurity.

Take the beginning swimmer, for instance, who is frightened by water. The only way he'll ever overcome his fear of water is to swim in it. So he progresses, step by step, from the shallow to the deeper areas until he is finally able to swim without fear in water over his head.

Now take yourself, for example. Are you afraid to meet people? Then go out of your way to do so. Soon you'll see that your fear was completely unjustified. Are you afraid to speak to a group of people? If so, stand up and talk every chance you get. Here's how Mildred Rogers overcame her fear of speaking to people and making conversation with them.

"I was even afraid to invite my friends in for fear I wouldn't be able to talk with them," Mildred says. "But after listening to your talk at our church, I took the plunge and held a block coffee call for a dozen of my neighbors day before yesterday. It was a great success. I had no trouble at all keeping the conversation going. All I really needed to do was just do it. Thanks so much for your help."

You can do exactly as Mildred did. Just do the things you fear to do, and you, too, will gain the power to do it. You'll quickly overcome your fear.

How to Conquer the Fear of Solving a Problem and Making a Decision

Although the previous three steps show you how to get rid of fear, I wanted to cover the fear of solving a problem and making a decision individually, for I know, without a doubt, this one drives more people up the wall than anything else. Not knowing what to do or when to do it is one of the most frustrating situations I can think of.

So I want to give you the format I've developed over the years to help me solve my own problems so you can make sound and timely decisions yourself. This format can also be helpful if you have people working for you. Show them this problem solving and decision making process, too. It will pay you rich dividends by saving you valuable time, money, and wasted effort.

Sometimes a person becomes confused about when a decision should be made. The answer is ever so simple whenever there is a problem to be solved. If there is no problem to be solved, then no action is necessary.

Now let me give you the outline you can follow to solve your problems so you can make a sound and logical decision without fear. Then I'll discuss each point with you individually.

1. Recognize the problem.
2. Make an estimate of the situation.
   a) Find out the exact cause of the problem.
   b) Determine all the possible solutions.
   c) Compare and evaluate the possible solutions.
   d) Make a decision; select the best solution.
3. Take the appropriate action; put your solution into effect.

Recognize the Problem

When does a problem exist? If it's a personal problem, then a good rule of thumb to follow is that whenever some aspect of your life has become unmanageable, you have a problem. For instance, if you smoke and want to quit, but can't, no doubt about it, you have a problem. A specific part of your life has become unmanageable.

In your dealings with other people, you have a problem whenever an incident occurs or conditions exist that adversely affect your relationships with them. If you have people working for you, then the problem could be one of morale, esprit, discipline, or job efficiency.

Make an Estimate of the Situation

Before you try to solve your problem, you should clearly and concisely define its exact nature: who is involved; what are the circumstances; when, where, and how did the problem occur. You can make a logical and orderly estimate of the situation by (1) finding the exact cause of the problem, (2) determining all the possible solutions, (3) comparing and evaluating the possible solutions, (4) selecting the best solution.

Find Out the Exact Cause of the Problem

Once you've determined the exact nature of your problem, you need then to determine *why* and *how* it arose and to ascertain all the relevant facts that bear on the problem.

You can assemble these facts in a variety of ways: by asking questions, by keeping your eyes and ears open, by researching the subject. If certain parts of the problem cannot be substantiated by facts, then you'll have to make some sound and logical assumptions.

Determine All the Possible Solutions

After you've determined the basic underlying cause or causes of your problem, you should next consider all the possible solutions to it. Don't rule out a solution on the first examination. Even if it later proves to be entirely worthless, a tentative solution may contain or suggest ideas of value. The more solutions you look over, the better your final solution is likely to be.

Compare and Evaluate the Possible Solutions

In evaluating the solutions you've picked, first compare the advantages of each one with its own disadvantages. Sometimes the disadvantages will so far outweigh the advantages that you'll have to discard the solution and not give it any further consideration.

After you've compared the advantages of each solution with its own disadvantages, then compare the merits of one solution against the merits of another so you can finally decide which one is the best.

Be careful not to let prejudice or personal preference influence your considerations. Remember that if you jump to conclusions, you will often create a more serious problem than the one you're trying to solve.

Make a Decision: Select the Best Solution

After you've checked and compared each solution with all the others, then you must make up your mind. You must make a decision and select the solution you feel will best solve your problem for you.

Your solution may be one of the single solutions you've previously considered, or it could be a combination of two or more of these possible solutions.

Take the Appropriate Action; Put Your Solution into Effect

Now put the solution you have chosen into effect, using the particular techniques that are appropriate to your own individual personality. Do not be satisfied with merely initiating the action. Your success will usually depend upon your ability and your willingness to supervise and check the results of your corrective action. One of the most significant factors of your success will be your ability to select and vigorously carry out an effective course of action.

4

How to Know When, Where, and on Whom to Use Your Miracle People Power

In Chapter 4, you'll learn how to be selective in your target. You'll find out how important it is for you to pinpoint the exact person who can help you get what you want, who can answer your questions, or who can help you solve your problems.

You see, you cannot succeed in life, either in business or socially, without the help of others. If you want to get ahead, you must get the right people on your side.

One of the best ways to do that is to use your miracle people power to influence and control, to master and dominate, certain key individuals—specific persons who can help you achieve that success. It's up to you to find out which people can help you the most.

This, then, should be your first goal: to discover which people can help you get what you want. When you do that, you'll be able to benefit tremendously by concentrating your attention only on those people who can help you achieve your goals.

Don't spend your valuable time and energy on someone who cannot help you get what you want. If you concentrate your attention on the wrong person, all your efforts will be wasted.

Instead, locate the person who can help you, the one who can get the job done for you, no matter who that person is. You might discover he's the janitor, just as Robert J. Underwood, the manager of the Lee Industries Kansas City Plant, did.

"We were having a tremendous problem with waste," Mr. Underwood says. "Our profit margin was steadily dropping and we seemed to have more going out the back door as scrap than we had going out the front door to be sold.

"The production superintendent was raising the devil with all the section supervisors, but he couldn't seem to get any accurate figures from them as to which section was at fault. They were all too busy trying to blame each other for the excessive waste.

"And I couldn't get any straight answers from the people who should've had them either. Then I remembered something I'd heard from a large department store owner one time. 'If you really want to know where your profit's going,' he told me, 'ask the janitor.'

"So I did just that. I called in the night janitor. In a matter of moments, I was able to find out which sections were generating the most scrap. Then I was able to solve my problem."

If you want to increase your miracle people power, then you, too, must do as Mr. Underwood did. You must find the person who knows the answers and who can help you get what you want. When you do,

YOU'LL GAIN THESE BENEFITS

How to Save Your Time

When you find the right person, the one who has the answers to your questions or the one who can solve your problems, you'll save a great deal of time. The time you spend in pinpointing the person who can help you is not wasted; it is an investment that will pay you rich dividends. For instance, there's a saying among successful salesmen that goes like this: *Sell the secretary on seeing her boss. Sell him on buying your product.*

Ask any successful person what his greatest problem is, and he will no doubt tell you, "Not enough time in the day to get things done." And if you're like most people, you will have that same complaint. But you can solve that problem when you concentrate your efforts on the individual who can get the job done for you. Don't waste your time on the person who can't help you.

How to Save Your Energy

Strange as it might sound at first, *it takes more energy to fail than it does to succeed.* If you exert your efforts and your energy on the wrong person, you'll get nowhere. You'll only wear yourself out.

No matter how many persons you work with or how many are in the group you want to influence and control, it's important that you locate the key people before you do anything else. You'll get the results you want when you do. Knowing who the pivot people are is a must when you need action and you need it right now. They can get that action for you when and where you most need it.

How to Control More People at Once

When you know who the key people are in a group, you'll find you can control many people through just a few. You don't have to personally control every person in the entire group by yourself to be successful. But you can influence dozens of people—yes, even hundreds—through just a few key people.

Take any PTA, church group, or town council, for instance. If you have a suggestion, a measure of some sort you want passed, a change you want made, don't waste your time talking to everyone. Find the key people who are interested in your proposal and let them do some of that talking for you. Get those key individuals on your side first; the rest will automatically follow.

TECHNIQUES YOU CAN USE TO GAIN THE BENEFITS

How to Pinpoint the People Who Are Really Important to You

Have you ever sat down and made up a list of the people in your life who are actually important to you? If you haven't, then you ought to do so right now, for you really should know which people can help you.

When you get through with your list, you'll probably have no more than a dozen or so names on it. You'll no doubt put down the name of your boss and maybe even the name of the man he works for, too. You could have the names of some of the associates you work with, important customers or clients, your husband or wife, maybe even the preacher or the banker.

And if you have people who work for you, I'm sure some of their names will be there, too, for a great many times, what they do or do not do can make you or break you as Dale Vance, a line supervisor with Westinghouse, well knows.

"If you're a production supervisor as I am, you must really know the people who work for you," Dale says. "You must know which ones are most important to you—which ones are the key individuals you can depend on to get the job done. Those are the people you want to put in your most sensitive spots—your critical positions—so they can watch your most vulnerable areas for you.

"By the same token, you want to know who your potential trouble makers are so you can keep them away from sensitive jobs where they can harm you. Those people are also extremely important to you, too, although in a much different way. I've seen the careers of young management people wrecked because they failed to realize this."

When you make up a list of names, then, ask yourself these basic questions:

1. *Why* is this person so important to me?
2. *What* can he do to *help* me?
3. *How* can he help me achieve my goals?
4. *What* can he do to *harm* me?
5. *How* could he keep me from attaining my goals?
6. *How* can I "use" him to help me succeed?

How These People Can Be of Service to You

One of the best ways you can "use" these individuals who are important to you is to pick their brains for your own benefit. For instance, chances are your boss didn't get to be boss just by pure dumb luck. He must have had something on the ball to get where he is.

So ask questions that will give him a chance to impart some of his knowledge to you. And he'll be glad to do that. Remember, the moment you ask a person for his opinion, you've made him feel important, and he can't help but tell you what you want to know.

And the same thing applies to the people who work for you. Pick their brains, too. Just because that person works under you doesn't mean that you're smarter than he is in every area. You can learn from him, too, if you'll just ask questions and be courteous and patient enough to listen to his answers.

"Every person I meet is smarter than I am in some way, and I can learn something helpful from him if I'll just force my ego to step aside so I can listen to him," says Roy Allen. "Like when our house was being built, I'd go by every day and watch the progress. The third morning the foreman said, 'Coming by to inspect again?' 'No,' I said. 'Just to look. I don't know how to inspect for I don't know anything about the construction business. Perhaps you could help me.'

"Well, he jumped at the chance to show off his knowledge to me. He explained each step as construction went along and told me why they were doing everything they did. I know I have a better built house than I'd have had otherwise for that foreman had to live up to the good reputation I gave him when I asked him to help me."

How to Cultivate the Friendship of the Right People

Not only does it make good sense to pinpoint the key people who can help you achieve your goals and become successful, but it's also a wise move on your part if you can also associate with them since they can help you get ahead.

At the same time, it makes no sense to me to cultivate the friendship of those who can do nothing for you. Why try to grow a crop of weeds? At first glance, you might disagree with this idea, but if you think it over carefully, I know you'll see what I'm driving at.

For instance, would you go out of your way to associate with the town drunk just because he was your high school classmate or your fraternity brother? I doubt it very much. In short, if you want to be successful, ask the successful man how it's done. Don't ask the failure. He won't be able to help you, unless you can learn from him what not to do.

How to Identify the Key People in Groups

In every group of people, you will always find certain key individuals who seem to naturally take over. I call them pivot people, for the action of the entire group will hinge or pivot upon what these key individuals say or do.

You can spot the pivot people easily for they will always be in the center of the action. They do not stand on the sidelines, just looking on. They are not spectators. They insist on getting into the act. Unlike so many people, they do want to get involved.

A pivot person will be the kind who automatically takes charge in some tragedy, say, for instance, an auto accident. He'll send someone to call for an ambulance and the police. He'll appoint someone else to direct traffic. He'll see that the injured people receive first aid.

This kind of person seems to be pushed by an inner urge for action. He has an internal drive to keep things moving along at a fast clip. He is always "chomping at the bit" to get things done. This kind of person will be able to harness his physical drive to solve mental tasks, too. For instance, he'll have that natural ability to take a good idea—either his own or someone else's—and ramrod it, promote it, or sell it to the group.

It matters not what kind of group it is—PTA, city council, school board, church group, employees in a department or a section—certain individuals always seem to be able to influence and control the entire group. If you can identify and recognize these key people, you will be able to master and dominate the entire group through them.

Although no two pivot people act alike, most of them have at least one, and sometimes more, of these particular characteristics or tendencies.

1. A pivot person will be a problem solver.
2. He tends to be an authoritative figure.
3. He possesses great drive, stamina, and endurance.
4. He is knowledgeable in a broad range of subjects.
5. He has a good memory.

6. He is an independent thinker.
7. He strives constantly to improve the system.

Now let's take up these characteristics one at a time in some detail.

Skill in Solving Problems

A pivot person almost always is able to come up with a workable solution to the problem. One of the hardest parts of solving any problem is simply getting started on it. That's why this kind of key personality can be so important to you. He'll often have several suggestions for solving your problems. His ideas may not always work every time, but he is able to get things moving in a bogged-down situation, and that's really important. He can usually help you get action from the group when you need it most.

Acting with Authority

A pivot person tends to stand out in any group. His manner, his bearing, his way of speaking all attract attention. He tends to take command of any situation, no matter what it is. Without appearing to force himself on others, a pivot person seems to just naturally assume authority and take over the leadership of the group.

"You can usually spot the pivot man in a group by watching the way others turn to him for guidance," says Melvin Bruce, a foreman with General Electronics in Houston, Texas. "For example, a supervisor issues an order, turns his back, and walks away.

"Immediately all the employees gather around one individual to get his opinion. He speaks; they listen. Then they go back to work and carry out the supervisor's order. But not until they get the unofficial go-ahead from the informal leader of the group."

Having Great Drive, Stamina, and Endurance

A key individual has the endurance, the drive, and the stamina to see things through to the end. He is able to stick to a job and finish it when others want to give up. If you're looking for someone to put on a long-term project or a project that has a multiplicity of details, he could be just the person you want to accomplish the job for you to its successful completion, especially if the goal to be reached is well worthwhile.

Knowledgeable in a Broad Range of Subjects

One of the best persons to have around in a tough situation will be the one who has a vast range of interests and broad general knowledge—especially when you're looking for new ideas to solve a problem. You see, new ideas usually spring from old ones so the person with this broad range of knowledge has the background and the potential for coming up with them.

Possessing a Good Memory

A good memory is important to the acquisition and retention of this knowledge. A key individual's good memory can be of great value to you when you need a quick solution to a pressing problem. The kind of person who can remember how a similar problem was solved last year can be invaluable to you in a crisis. A man with a good memory may be the first one to come up with information or help when you really need it in a hurry.

An Independent Thinker

A key individual will be an independent creative thinker. He will not be a *yes man*. The famous John D. Rockefeller recognized how important a creative thinker was to his organization. One day he stopped at the desk of a busy young paper-shuffling junior executive.

After watching this dynamo of energy for a few minutes, Mr. Rockefeller put his hand on the young man's shoulder and said, "You shouldn't work so hard. Let your secretary handle all that paperwork. Then you can sit back and think up new ways to help Standard Oil make more money. That's what executives are paid for."

And when I see the price of gasoline and oil, I think this young man must have taken Mr. Rockefeller's advice.

Striving Constantly to Improve "The System"

A pivot person can often be recognized by the way he hates the routine way of doing things. He refuses to accept the status quo and is constantly looking for better ways of doing things. He's the kind of person you want around to help you for he can often solve your problems before they happen.

Making Your Miracle People Power Work Every Time

You must know when to use your miracle people power to get the results you want. You must always time it right. If you want your wife, your husband, your boss, your employees, your prospect to listen to you when you speak . . . if you expect them to do as you say and to do what you want them to do, then always time the favor that you're asking of them.

If you don't use the proper timing, you won't get the results you want. You'd be like an Iowa farmer who plants his corn and oats in December and then wonders why his crops never grow. Or you'd be as implausible as the person who applauds the trumpet player after he plays taps at a military funeral. Improper timing with anything can make you look foolish.

So time your requests for that mink coat, those golf clubs, that raise in pay, your employees' extra effort, that sale to your customer —and you'll find that you'll always be able to use your miracle people power to get what you want. It'll work on everybody every time—no exceptions—just as long as you time it right.

"To everything there is a season, and a time to every purpose under heaven." Ecclesiastes, 3:11.

5

Use This Miracle People
Power Tool and Get
Instantaneous Results

In this chapter on miracle people power, you'll learn how to use a power tool that will bring you instantaneous results. This miracle people power tool can be used successfully on rebellious teen-agers, nagging wives, unhappy husbands, stubborn employees, dissatisfied customers, and even hardened criminals. People will not only like you—they'll love you when you use this miracle power tool on them.

How Ralph Elliott Uses This Powerful Tool
to Calm an Angry Employee

Ralph Elliott is a top-notch employee-relations expert for a large Los Angeles radio and television manufacturer. He uses this miracle people power tool to handle the grievances of an angry employee and to keep harmonious relations between management and labor in the company.

"When a person comes to me with a problem, I always listen to his story from beginning to end without saying a single word," Ralph says. "I never interrupt him—not even once. I let him get it all off his chest. That's the first thing he wants: someone who will listen patiently to him; someone who'll lend him a sympathetic ear.

"After he's finished with his story, I tell him I can't help but agree with him after looking at it from his point of view. I also tell him I understand how he feels about this problem, and that if I were in his position, I'd probably look at it the same way, too.

"Now I've taken a lot of his anger away by first listening to him and then by agreeing with him. He wasn't prepared for that at all. He came in looking for a fight and suddenly finds that I'm his friend—not his enemy. Now I add the finishing touch by asking him what he wants me to do.

"He's really floored by now. Most employee relations managers *tell* a man what the company will do for him. Not me. I know I can't get anywhere with him that way. So I never tell him what I'm going to do about his problem. I always ask him what he wants me to do.

"If it's something I can fix, I take steps to do so, of course. But often the man is *already satisfied* when I ask him what he wants me to do, for I've had men look at me in astonishment and say, 'I really don't know. Nothing, I guess. I just wanted someone to listen to my side for a change. You've done that for me. If you can just keep this from happening again, I'll be satisfied.'

"You see, when you ask a person what he wants you to do, you'll find you satisfy both his psychological and his 'real' problems at the same time. I never cease to be amazed at how much can be accomplished with that one little question: *'What would you like me to do?'*

"I always finish the interview by saying that I will do my level best to keep this difficulty from coming up again. And I tell him to make sure to bring any problem—I never use the word *complaint*—to me at any time, no matter how small or trivial it might seem to be, for I'm sincerely willing to listen whenever he needs help again.

"So he leaves, happy and completely satisfied with an answer I never gave him. You see, he supplied his own answer. All I had to do was listen. To listen patiently and quietly with compassion and understanding is the most powerful tool you can ever use on an angry person. It will literally work miracles for you."

You, too, can calm down an angry person just as Ralph does. I want you to remember the exact steps he uses, so let me quickly summarize them for you:

1. Listen to the angry person's story from beginning to end without saying a single word.

2. Tell him you can't help but agree with him after looking at the problem from his point of view. (If you can't say you *agree*—then say you *understand*.)
3. Ask him what he wants you to do.
4. Tell him you'll do your best to keep this same problem from coming up again.
5. Say you'll always be ready to listen to him any time in the future if he ever needs your help again.

Besides learning how to calm down an angry person with this miracle people power tool, here are some more—

BENEFITS YOU'LL GAIN

You'll Gain Many True Friends

Listen to another person and you'll open the door to a lasting friendship. People will always confide in—and trust—someone who listens to them with sincerity. So encourage people to talk about themselves; they'll love you for it.

You'll Gain Much Valuable Information

Get a person to talk about the three most important things in his life (which will usually be himself, his children, and his possessions) and you'll learn an immense amount of information about him that will be extremely useful to you.

People Will Admire and Respect You

People admire and respect someone who has the courtesy to listen to their opinions. By the same token, they thoroughly dislike the person who talks only of himself and his own desires. So if you want to gain the respect and the admiration of others, then pay attention to them and listen to what they say.

You'll Strengthen Your Powers of Persuasion

Listening is one of the finest tools you can use to sharpen your own powers of persuasion. You see, when you listen to what a person says, you can find out what he wants and then show him the easiest way to get it.

You'll Improve Your Own Personal Efficiency

Besides increasing your miracle people power with others by listening to them, you'll also be able to improve your own work. Poor communication leads to misunderstanding, arguments, and an inefficient operation. But good communication means you'll get things done right the first time. And getting things done right the first time means you'll save yourself both time and energy.

TECHNIQUES YOU CAN USE TO GAIN THESE BENEFITS

If you're going to use this miracle people power tool properly to get the results you want, you must get yourself in the right frame of mind. There are four specific actions you can take to make sure you do have the correct attitude. These are *learn to listen with everything you've got . . . forget yourself . . . practice patience . . . be concerned.*

Learn to Listen with Everything You've Got

I know of no faster way to insult another person or to hurt his feelings than to cut him off when he's trying to tell you something. Ever have someone do that to you? Ever try to tell your boss your side of it only to have him turn his back on you, or walk away from you, or tell you to hurry up and get it over with? I've had it happen to me; I'm sure you have, too. You know how deeply it can hurt when other people don't listen to you, so don't be guilty of such improper conduct yourself.

And if you have children, you should realize they feel the same way if you brush them aside, ignore them, refuse to listen to them, or pay no attention to their problems.

How Dr. Farrell Gets Results with This Miracle People Power Tool

Here's what Dr. Ronald J. Farrell, a Denver psychologist and head of the Farrell & Associates Psychological Guidance Center, says about how important it is to listen to people.

"In our clinic, we find that the counselor most likely to get results is the one who has mastered the art of paying attention to the patient and listening deeply to his problems," Dr. Farrell says. "The reason for this is extremely clear. You see, it matters not whether we're young or old, happy or sad, rich or poor, each one of us craves attention. We want someone who will really listen to us.

"Recently a couple brought a 15 year old girl to me. She'd been a runaway from home. Her parents had put her in a juvenile detention center for a week and had threatened to send her to a girls' reformatory until she was 17 unless she straightened out. But the judge of the juvenile court wanted me to talk to them first before he made his final decision.

" 'We give her everything,' her mother complained to me. 'I don't know what's wrong with her; she never listens to anything we say.'

"But when I talked to the girl, I heard quite a different story. 'My parents don't care about me,' she said. 'We never do anything together. My mother never looks at me when I talk to her; she just keeps on reading her magazine or watching TV. My father's always nagging at me about money and clothes, but he never listens when I try to explain anything to him. He just says he's not interested and for me not to bother him.'

"I told her parents they should pay some attention to their daughter and start listening to her so they could help her with her problems. Thank God, they did, and things are working out much better for all of them now.

"You see, when you don't listen to someone—you reject them. But when you do listen to them—you accept them. Rejection hurts; acceptance heals. It's as simple as that."

When you listen to the person with everything you've got, you must put aside your own interests, your own pleasures, and your own preoccupations, at least for the time being. For those few moments of time, you must concentrate your attention 100 percent on the other person and listen deeply to what he is saying. You must listen to him with all the intensity and awareness that you can command. And to be able to do that, you must. . . .

Forget Yourself Completely

If you're going to use this miracle people power tool to get the instantaneous results you're after, you must forget yourself completely. You must force your own ego to step aside and give way to another person's ego instead.

This is hard to do at first for all of us are self-centered most of the time. To me—I am the center of everything; the world revolves around me. But as far as you are concerned—you are the center of everything; the world revolves around you. Almost all of us are constantly seeking to be the center of attraction. Most of our waking moments are spent in trying to gain status of some sort.

But if you want to achieve miracle power with people, that is exactly what you must not do. You will have to train your attention hungry ego to take a back seat for a change. You'll have to stop trying to be in the spotlight and let it fall on the other person for a while.

Will it pay you dividends to forget yourself long enough to listen to the other person? It most certainly will, according to Bert Wheeler, the founder and president of Wheeler's Discount Markets, a midwest grocery chain.

> "I've found that if I can forget myself, my status, and my self-importance long enough to listen to some of my employees, I can pick up a lot of good new ideas," Bert says. "But I can't learn anything from my people if I'm more concerned about my status, who and what I am, than with what they want to tell me.
>
> "For instance, I can think of all sorts of recommendations I failed to accept in the past just because I thought I was too high and mighty to listen to George, the stock room clerk, or to Sally, the cashier.

"Today, I know better. I've learned that all sorts of good ideas can come from the people who are actually doing the job, because they know more about their jobs than anyone else does. All I need do is forget myself long enough to keep my ears open and listen to them."

Practice Patience

I know it's hard to be patient when you're in a hurry and the other person insists on telling you every single minute detail. A fellow who used to work for me was like that. He nearly drove me up the wall sometimes and I felt like reaching in his mouth and dragging the words out faster, but by being patient and hanging on until he was through, I was usually amply rewarded, for his ideas were sound and logical. Oh, once in a while I had to listen to some nonsense, but all in all, his good ideas far outweighed his useless ones.

"Once in a while, you can speed up this process by asking the person to give you a brief oral summary and to put all the details in writing," says Gene Gordon, a design engineer with Radiation, Inc., a subsidiary of Harris Intertype, in Palm Bay, Florida. "But that isn't always possible so if you don't want to run the risk of missing something really important and worthwhile, you'll simply have to develop the patience to hear the person out."

One of the best ways I've found to practice patience is not to criticize and offer snap judgments no matter how pushed I am for time. It's always better to sleep on it first before you offer an opinion, especially if it's one that could destroy the other person's ego, dignity, and self-respect. Useless criticism is not the way to achieve miracle people power with anyone.

A great many times patience is simply a matter of waiting, watching, listening, standing by quietly until the person you are trying to help works out the answer to his own problem. That's precisely how Ralph Elliott gained his reputation as a top-notch employee relations expert, remember?

Be Concerned

Why is it that groups such as Alcoholics Anonymous, Synanon, and Weight Watchers succeed in helping people when other more conventional methods fail? Because the people in those groups learn to listen with everything they've got to the person who needs help. They forget themselves completely in the service of others. They are patient and understanding—they never criticize.

But above all, they are deeply concerned about the welfare of their fellow human being. As a result, they are able to achieve a group people power that literally does work miracles for that person who needs such specialized help.

If you feel you can achieve miracle people power at the expense of the other person, or without being concerned for the other person and his welfare, let me tell you right now: you're terribly wrong. Your miracle people power must benefit the other person, too, or it will not work for you at all.

So you must learn to be deeply concerned about the other person before you can ever expect this miracle power tool to work for you. There's very little use of listening to a person, forgetting yourself, or practicing patience unless you really are concerned about that person and his welfare.

And when you are concerned about him, you'll have compassion for him. You'll be willing to share his pain and his sorrow. You will want to listen to his problems and help him overcome his difficulties. To be concerned about the other person is the basic foundation of all deep and lasting human relationships. It is the heart of all friendship and a real key to miracle people power.

NINE TIPS ON HOW TO USE THIS MIRACLE PEOPLE POWER TOOL EFFECTIVELY

1. **Find Areas of Interest in What the Speaker Is Saying.** Ask yourself, "What is he saying that I can use? What new idea is he offering that is of value to me? Is he reporting any worthwhile or workable procedure? Is he presenting a problem that I can help him to solve?"

2. **How to Turn on the Power Switch Immediately.** If you're going to listen, the other person has to talk. If he's at all reluctant to do so, ask him questions to get him started. Structure your questions so they cannot be answered with *yes* or *no*. Instead, say, "What about this?" "How about that?" "What's your opinion on this point?" "Why do you feel this way?"

3. Make Sure You Understand. A good way to do this is to summarize back to the person. For example, "Jerry, let me see if I understand what you've said correctly. You say you like the idea and you'd go ahead with it but you can't afford the money right now. Is that about right?" If it is, the person can say so. If it's not, then he can clarify the point for you by further explanation.

4. Judge the Content . . . Not the Delivery. Don't waste your time mentally criticizing the person's mistakes in grammar, inflection, voice quality, style of delivery, and so on. Concentrate on *what* he's saying—not *how* he's saying it.

5. Don't Interrupt. Give the person a chance to finish. Don't jump in and interrupt the moment you hear a point with which you don't agree. Hold your fire until he's completely through. Then if it is absolutely necessary, you can have your turn.

6. Listen for Ideas—Not Words. Don't try to pull a sentence or two out of context and use that to criticize or tear down the speaker. Listen for the central theme of what he's saying and follow it through to the end.

7. Work at It. It is not easy to become a good listener. In fact, it takes a lot of hard work to develop good listening habits. You must practice to keep your mind from wandering. And you can't fool the speaker for long. He'll soon know if you're really listening to him or if you're just faking it.

8. Avoid Physical and Mental Distractions. It's tough to listen closely if your speaker is competing with a radio, some machinery, or other people. Do your best to get rid of all mental and physical distractions so you can concentrate fully on what he's saying.

9. Stretch Your Mind. It's no longer safe to say that anything is impossible. What man can conceive—man can apparently do. The main obstacle to overcome is believing an idea isn't possible. And don't close your mind to a new idea just because you didn't think of it first. It's just possible that the old way of doing things isn't the best way after all.

6

How to Use Miracle People Power to Get Your Own Way Every Time

You can use one of two basic methods to get your own way every time. One method is by the use of fear. You can scare a person into doing what you want him to do by threatening him with the loss of his job, suspension, demotion, a fine, loss of privileges, and so on. The disadvantages of this "do it my way or else" method so far outweigh the advantages, if there actually are any, I will not consider it any further.

The second method you can use to get your own way every time is to persuade the other person to your way of thinking so that he will *want* to do what you want him to do. I think it goes almost without saying that this is by far the more preferable method for it is the only one that offers any lasting results.

How Vince Ireland Learned to Get His Own Way Every Time

"When I first went to work in the plant here, I was given the job of straightening up a department that had been completely demoralized by the previous foreman," Vince Ireland says. "He'd been from the old school that believed in pushing people around and using threats to get the job done. He ran his department as if he were a cop handing out traffic tickets. But the louder he yelled, the worse things got, so finally the company let him go.

"I figured that if I didn't want to end up like him, the best thing for me to do was the exact opposite of what he'd done. I wasn't an expert in applied psychology or human relations, but I'd just finished reading a book called *The 22 Biggest Mistakes Managers Make And How To Correct Them*,[1] and from the looks of his department and the reports I'd heard about it, that foreman had made every single one of them.

"So I tried to do the exact opposite of what he had done. I used the corrective measures the author recommended in that book. Just for instance, instead of yelling at people when they made a mistake, I showed them how to do the job properly. Instead of using harsh criticism, I motivated a person to do better by praising him for his efforts. Or instead of threatening an individual with the loss of his job, I helped him improve his work methods so he could make more incentive pay.

"These are only a few examples to show how I was able to get what I wanted every time from my people without yelling at them, bulldozing my way over the top of them, or using threats to scare them into doing things my way."

I'm sure you can see from what Vince says that the use of fear tactics to get what you want is a complete waste of time. Whenever you're tempted to use threats to get what you want, just remember that *fear always leads to hate*. If you give a person reason to fear you, you'll also cause him to hate you.

In this chapter on miracle people power, then, I want to give you some more of the techniques Vince used so you can put the second method to work for yourself. Then the person with whom you're dealing will *want* to do what you want him to do.

That, of course, is the real secret of getting what you want or getting your own way every time. Whenever people are glad to do what you want them to do, and when they're anxious to do it for you, then you've got your miracle people power zooming along at its peak efficiency.

---

[1] James K. Van Fleet, *The 22 Biggest Mistakes Managers Make and How to Correct Them* (West Nyack, New York, Parker Publishing Co., 1973).

Since the benefits you'll gain when you get what you want every time will be entirely dependent upon your own individual situation and circumstances, I'm going to move right on to the—

TECHNIQUES YOU CAN USE
TO GET YOUR OWN WAY EVERY TIME

Use This Technique: You'll Always Get Your Own Way

Let's say you want something done a certain way. You can either tell a person to do it your way, or else you can use tact and diplomacy to keep away from the acute angle, come in through the side door, and get things done the way you want them done without the other person ever realizing what actually happened. How can you do that? Easy. *Just let the other fellow think the whole project was his own idea.* Here's an example of how that works:

"I've found that the best way to get a job done is to let the other person think it was all his own idea," says Kelly Riebold, a supervisory specialist with General Electric's Springfield, Missouri, plant. "Actually, I've yet to meet the individual who isn't susceptible to that kind of an approach.

"Take Glen over there, for example. If I want to get something done my way without any argument, I'll say to him very confidentially on Friday, 'Glen, I've been thinking about shifting the number four machine to that spot over there. I believe we can cut our line production time quite a bit if we do. I wish you'd think it over and give me your feeling on it as soon as you can. I'd like to have your opinion on the switch.'

"Well, it never fails. On Monday, Glen will come rushing into my office and say, 'Kelly, I just had the most terrific idea over the weekend. Let's shift the number four machine over to this point. I know we can speed up our production if we do.'

"This system beats the dickens out of telling people what to do. People don't like to do what they're told to do; they like to do things their own way. And this method works every time. I get what I want; Glen gets the credit that he wants.

"Why, he thinks every single improvement in the department is a result of his ideas. I don't mind. After all, he does what I want him to do; he just doesn't realize it. I get my own way every time and that's all I'm after. Glen can have all the credit he wants."

If you've never used this technique before, do so now. It'll work every time on everyone. A person is always anxious to do things his own way and carry out his own ideas. All you have to do is plant your idea in his mind in such a way that he comes to think of it as his very own. Just plant the seed—let him harvest the crop. Do that and you'll be able to get your own way every time.

How to Make Sure He Can't Refuse What You Ask

Let's say you want a certain job done. You could tell a person to do it, but you know full well that everyone instinctively rebels when you give them orders. So how do you handle it? Like this: Instead of telling an individual what to do, *ask him to show you how to do it.* Let me give you an example of how that technique works:

> "One of the toughest problems the average small businessman has to solve is cutting his costs and reducing his overhead," Dale Jeffries says. "And when your net profit is figured in pennies as it is in the restaurant business, you've got to cut corners every chance that you get.
> "I've found it doesn't do any good for me to preach to my cooks or yell at my waitresses to cut costs. Nor can I get them to reduce waste by ordering them to do so. But I do know from experience I can get my own way every time when I ask them to show me how to do it.
> "The minute I ask my people to show me how to cut costs and reduce my overhead, they go to work on the problem for me. And they do come up with workable solutions most of the time. Then all I have to do is ask them to put their own ideas into effect for *people will always support what they themselves suggest.* I've yet to have a person refuse to help me when I ask him to show me how to get the job done."

This procedure can also be used in your house. Suppose you'd like to cut down on your household bills. Don't arbitrarily tell your wife that she has to reduce her grocery budget or else. Instead, ask her to show you how to do it.

Or let's say your monthly utility bill is far too high. You could issue a direct order to everyone never to touch the thermostat, to turn off every light when not in use, and to limit the shower time to three minutes. But I doubt seriously if these methods will work—at least for very long. Instead, I'd recommend you use the procedure I found to be highly effective in my own home.

One year we'd had an unusual amount of unanticipated expenditures—doctor bills, hospital expenses, and the like—and I was trying desperately to cut down everywhere. Our monthly utility bill was a sore spot with me for it was especially high. For one reason, our children thought they should be able to walk around the house in shorts in the dead of winter and be prefectly warm and comfortable. And our youngest son had the bad habit of standing in the shower until every bit of hot water was completely gone.

I called a family conference, explained the financial situation, and asked them to tell me how we could cut down on our utility bill.

"Well, dad, we could wear a sweater around the house," my daughter said. "Then we could keep the thermostat at a lower setting and that would help a little bit."

"Yeah, and you could turn off the lights and the TV in your room every time you go out," her older brother said. "I'll bet that would cut dad's electric bill at least 10 dollars every month."

They presented still other ideas and at the end of our family get-together I said, "Good. You've all shown me how we can do it and I appreciate your help. I'll accept all your suggestions and we'll put them all into operation at once."

The end result was we reduced our utility bill by $12.00 a month. Not only that, my children enjoyed the idea of being asked for advice and they volunteered more suggestions that helped us economize even further in other areas. I don't know about you, but in these days of ever increasing prices, every dollar is extremely important to me.

How to Get People to Do Things Your Way

If you're a member of management in business or industry, or if you own your own business, I know you'll be interested in increased production or sales, cutting down on loss or waste, and increasing your net profits. Do you know how you can get people to do things your own way so you can accomplish all this?

Well, the answer is really quite simple. You let them take part in the planning and the decision-making process as much as humanly possible. Today, management consultants call this procedure *job enrichment* and intimate that it's a brand-new technique to get the best out of people. But Jimmy Durante gave us the secret a long time ago when he said, "Everybody wants to get into the act."

Old or new, the technique does work. For instance, in Tulsa, Oklahoma, headquarters for Southwest Van Lines, Inc., a group of long distance drivers were complaining about the company's trucks. Front-end suspensions were faulty, tires wore out quickly, fuel consumption was high, and major engine breakdowns were commonplace.

Learning from the dispatcher that Southwest was planning to buy all new trucks, the drivers appointed senior driver George Meyers to go talk to the purchasing manager. Meyers asked if the drivers themselves could help draw up the specifications for the replacement fleet.

The purchasing manager got the go-ahead from the executive vice-president, L. W. Price, and Meyers and the rest of the drivers tackled the job enthusiastically. Every suggestion they made—including improved front-end suspensions, padded interiors, fog lights, and heated outside mirrors—was logical.

Mr. Price then wondered how driver performance would be affected if the company changed the practice of assigning each man a different truck for every trip, and instead let the drivers have the new trucks for themselves on a permanent basis. He asked the men and they voted for this new method unanimously. Maintenance costs promptly fell. Trucks no longer blew tires, ran out of fuel, or experienced costly engine failures.

Why? Mr. Price found the answer when he expressed surprise upon seeing a veteran driver, Dean Osborn, washing and waxing his truck on his off-duty time. Osborn's explanation was, "It's *my* truck now."

This idea of letting people take part in the planning and decision-making process works in the home, too. "I wanted my three daughters to help me with the meals and the housework without complaining about it," Pauline Kirby says. "So I let them plan all the meals, make up the grocery shopping list, and decide the house-work that's to be done each day.

"Of course, I have to give them some gentle guidance, but after all, they are still learning. But by letting them make the plans and carry out their own decisions, I'm teaching them to accept responsibility. Not only that, this method has helped us maintain a more harmonious family relationship in our home."

Just a quick word of caution now. Never try to get what you want at the other person's expense. If only you will benefit, your procedure won't work. Look back at the example of Southwest Van Lines, and you'll see how the company and the employees both benefited. So remember, to get people to do what you want them to do, you must make sure they get something worthwhile in return. Both parties have to benefit if you're going to get your own way every time.

When Nothing Else Works, Use This Technique

If you want to get your own way every time, then *throw down a challenge to get the results you're after*. When you do, you touch a man's competitive quick, and he'll rise to this stimulus when all else has failed. Let me give you an example to show you just how this technique works.

"I look at my ability to rouse the competitive spirit in a person as the greatest asset I possess," says Earl Lane, Vice-President in charge of manufacturing for the Dominion Corporation.

"One of our branch plants, which manufactures plastic and rubber parts for the rest of our corporation, was having all sorts of trouble meeting its production quota. I went down there to find out why. The plant manager gave me no answer; he couldn't put his finger on the problem. Nor could the production superintendent or his mill foreman. They all knew which department was at fault—but no one really knew why production was lagging so badly.

"I was determined to find the answer for myself. I had to, for the production in our other plants had slowed down because of a lack of these parts for their unit assemblies. We were in an extremely critical position for some of our best customers were threatening to cancel their orders and find another supplier. I had to find a solution to the problem and find it quick so I went right out to the production line to find my answer.

" 'How many units did your shift produce today?' I asked the supervisor.

" 'Three hundred,' he said.

"It was barely half his capacity. He knew it and so did I, but I said no more to him. Instead, I walked over to the mill department's bulletin board by the time clock. I tore a sheet of paper from my clipboard and tacked it up on the board. I wrote a big figure '3' on it. Then I turned my back on the supervisor and walked away.

"When the next shift came in, some of the men called their supervisor's attention to the number 3 on their bulletin board. Naturally, they wanted to know what it meant, and so did he. Not only was he told what it stood for, but he was also informed by the departing shift supervisor that it couldn't be topped. *That first supervisor was already rising to the bait.*

"But how wrong that day shift supervisor was," Mr. Lane says. "When he came back to work the next morning, he found the 3 had been crossed out and a new sheet of paper with a 5 on it was covering it up. *The second supervisor had also been hooked.*

"And so it went. By the time I left, that plant was exceeding its daily quota and was able to stockpile a 30 day supply just in case a real emergency came along. Costwise, it has risen from the least efficient plant in our corporation to the top one during the past year. And all because *I threw down a challenge to get results.*"

Now you don't have to be the vice-president of a big corporation to use this technique. I knew an army sergeant once who used it constantly to get better results from his platoon. I've seen it used successfully in the construction industry and in the retail business, especially by Sears Roebuck.

So next time you're appointed chairman for the annual Red Cross drive or the United Fund campaign, use it. You'll be absolutely amazed at the results you get.

Or use it on your children to improve their grades in school or to improve any performance of theirs. Or use it on your husband to spur him on to get that promotion he wants. The variety of situations in which you can use this technique to get your own way every time are virtually unlimited. All you need do is put your imagination to work.

How to Appeal to a Person's Emotions to Get Your Own Way Every Time

If you want a person to really listen to you, pay attention to you, and do what you say, then appeal to his emotions; get him emotionally involved. Sure you have to appeal to his logic and his common sense, but the average person does most things on impulse, on the way he *feels* about something at the time.

Look at Oral Roberts, for instance. Do you think he built Oral Roberts University in Tulsa, Oklahoma, by appealing to people's logic and reason? Not at all. He built it by appealing to people's emotions for their contributions, by telling them to give to God, and then to "expect a miracle every day."

Once there was a young man in a small New England town with a book—and an idea. The book had been written for people who wanted to get ahead and be successful. But letters and advertising offering this book for sale had left their prospects completely unimpressed—so much so that the original publisher of the work had failed. The young man had been the publisher's bookkeeper. He bought the plates and stock at the sale of the publisher's effects. No one else wanted them.

This young man was sure he could sell the book. He felt that a description of the book's contents, such as the former publisher had used in his letters and ads, was not the way to sell it. He felt strongly that the only way to sell the book was to appeal to the buyer's emotions. He had only $200 left after buying the plates and stock, but he followed his hunch and spent it all on new advertising.

From that small start he sold $2,000 worth of books by direct mail. He immediately reinvested that in more advertising and continued this way until he eventually made more than $2,000,000 in sales! His name was A. L. Pelton. The book was called *Power of Will*.

The point is, he sold those books by appealing not just to a man's logic and reason—but to his emotions with such phrases as "Five Days to Prove I can Raise Your Pay" and "A New Idea That Makes Men Rich."

And you can get your own way every time when you appeal to a person's emotions, too. Oh, you should appeal to his good judgment by all means. Give people a logical and sensible reason for doing what you want them to do.

But if you really want to influence people, if you want action from them, if you do want to get your own way every time, then appeal to one of their basic emotional drives. Just remember this thought:

THE HEAD NEVER HEARS 'TIL THE HEART HAS LISTENED.

7

How to Use Words That Will Double and Triple Your Miracle People Power

In Chapters 8 and 9, I'm going to show you *How to Put Miracle People Power into Everything You Say,* and *How to Write Letters that Are Loaded with Miracle People Power*.

However, before I cover these two highly beneficial chapters with you, I first want to give you some of the tools you'll need to make them work. The tools of communication are the words you use. How well you speak and write and how well you get your point across to your listener will depend entirely upon how selective you are in your choice of your words.

Surprising as it might seem to you at first, I am not going to ask you to increase your vocabulary by adding a lot of big words to it. To use a big word when a smaller one will do just as well is extremely unwise. You run the risk of losing the attention as well as the understanding of your reader or your listener.

Just for instance, look at the following examples: *Simians indigenous to Zamboanga are destitute of caudal appendages.* That sentence is entirely correct, but it is much more concrete, understandable, and to the point if you say, *Monkeys have no tails in Zamboanga.*

My own attitude about big words is simply this: Most of them are too cumbersome, pompous, and useless. As my high school English teacher, John W. Harlan, used to say, "A vocabulary of big words is much better for catching than it is for pitching."

To tell the truth, small words will say everything that big words will say and they will say them quite well. I myself try never to use a word of three or more syllables if a word with one or two will do.

So then, I'm going to show you how small one and two syllable words can make your speaking and writing abilities powerful and persuasive. In fact, you might even relearn some of the English language, as Gerald Thompson had to do.

How Gerald Thompson Rediscovered the English Language

"Even though I'd received my bachelor's degree in journalism from the University of Iowa, I had to rediscover the English language when I went to work for the Des Moines Register and Tribune," Gerald says. "Let me tell you how that happened.

"Following graduation, I went into the army to serve my required two years of active duty as a reserve officer. And that's where my troubles with the English language began, for the armed services have their own separate jargon which is usually called *federalese*.

"Federalese is the art of substituting pompous, abstract, and meaningless words for simple concrete ones. An expert in the use of federalese can confuse his reader, cloud and muddle the issue, and pass the buck indefinitely to someone else.

"I soon mastered this art of *obfuscation*. I learned to use fluently and with ease such words as *construct, fabricate, accomplish, perform, consummate,* and *effect* instead of *make* or *do*. I found that in the army you never *start* or *begin* anything. You always *initiate, commence,* or *inaugurate* it.

"Nor does the army simply *send* messages; it always *forwards, transmits,* or *communicates* them. And information is never *sent out* . . . it is *circulated, promulgated,* or *disseminated*. It is also against army custom to use such small words as *if, so, for,* and *but*. They must be replaced by such clumsy words and awkward phrases as *in the event that, due to the fact that, inasmuch as, on behalf of, notwithstanding the fact that, for the purpose of,* and so on.

"But when I left the army to come here as a newspaper man, all that had to change. The job of a reporter is not to *confuse,* but to *clarify*. To be able to do that, I had to learn the English language all over again."

BENEFITS YOU'LL GAIN

People Will Understand You

When you use simple one and two syllable words that everyone can understand, you lend precision and clarity to what you say. You reduce the possibility of being misunderstood. Not only is it important for you to speak and write so that you will be clearly understood, but also so that it will be impossible for you to be misunderstood.

You'll Get Things Done Right

When you use big words, they can often get in the way of what you really want to say. And when you're through, no one knows for sure exactly what you want him to do. But when you use small, specific, concrete words, you reduce the chances of misunderstanding and confusion. So if you want to get things done right, then use small words so everyone will know exactly what you want.

You'll Become a Clearer Thinker

It's all too easy to use vague, abstract words. But it takes some effort to find the correct words to take their place. For instance, you can use *machine* as a general term, but if you can, you should use the specific name of that machine, be it a crane or a bulldozer, a mimeograph or a typewriter. If you make yourself use the exact term when you speak or write, you'll force yourself to become a clearer thinker.

You'll Gain a Feeling of Power
and Confidence in Yourself

When you know the exact meaning of the words you use, you'll have a feeling of power and self-confidence. Instead of concentrating on the meaning of the words you use, you can devote all your attention to your message. That will let you become much more persuasive so you can really add miracle people power to your letters and to everything you say.

TECHNIQUES YOU CAN USE TO GAIN THE BENEFITS

How to Use Words that Have Zing and Punch

When you talk and write, use nouns and verbs—not adjectives and adverbs. This is not to say that adjectives and adverbs don't have their place, but if you use the correct nouns and right verbs to fully describe what you mean, you'll find that your need for additional descriptive words is greatly reduced.

"Active verbs are the most important words you can use to put color and movement into your writing and your conversation," says Roy Updike, a copywriter with Barstow & Associates in Salt Lake City.

"Verbs are the voice, not only of persuasion, but also of command," Mr. Updike goes on to say. "Active verbs, when used with the proper nouns, can make your advertising message vigorous, strong, and hard to resist.

"*Go buy our product right now!* is one of the most powerful phrases you can use to put your idea across."

Don't Use Nouns Made Out of Verbs

Good strong active verbs of motion can be ruined when you change them into abstract pompous nouns by adding *-ion, -ance, -ence,* or *-osity.* The most common ending you'll run into is *-ion.*

When you use these abstract nouns made out of verbs, you'll find you're forced to use weak passive verbs to support and carry them. It is practically impossible to use a strong and active one-syllable verb like *run, throw,* or *strike* when you have an abstract noun for the subject of your sentence.

If you find yourself using *disintegration* for *fall apart . . . penetration* for *break through . . . condescension* for *look down on . . . intervention* for *come between . . . discussion* for *talk about*—then it's time for you to clean house.

So keep your eyes open for such words as *examination, decision, preparation, performance, accomplishment, repetition, impression, situation,* and the like. Every single one of these abstract nouns is made out of a verb. If you do nothing more than cut most of the words that end with *-ion* out of your word usage, you'll do wonders for both your clarity and your style in your speaking and writing.

The best nouns to use for clear understanding are the names of people, places, and things. These are known as concrete nouns. Nouns that describe qualities and ideas are abstract. It is best to avoid these abstract nouns or limit their usage as much as possible.

Don't Smother Your Verbs

Simple straightforward active verbs can often be smothered with useless phrases. Look how the words *correct* and *have* are completely buried in this sentence: "It is requested that you take appropriate action to accomplish the *correction* of these records and that you transmit a request to your home office with a view toward *having* them make a similar *correction*." How much simpler and more understandable it would have been to say: "Please *correct* your records at once and *have* your home office *correct* theirs."

How to Use Simple Verbs that Mean What They Say

To help you get rid of abstract nouns and their passive verbs, I've made up a list of simple one and two syllable verbs you can use to describe nearly any action you can possibly think of. When you use these verbs, it is almost impossible to make their subject an abstract noun.

Don't look at this list as all-inclusive. Use it instead as a base, and add your own simple one and two syllable verbs to it as you go along.

Act	Carry	Drive	Help	Pick	Say	Stay	Touch
Aim	Cast	Drop	Hold	Pitch	See	Stick	Turn
Ask	Catch	Fall	Hurt	Play	Set	Strike	Walk
Bear	Come	Get	Keep	Poke	Shake	Take	Want
Blow	Crawl	Give	Lay	Pull	Show	Talk	Watch
Break	Cut	Go	Let	Push	Skip	Tear	Wear
Bring	Do	Hang	Look	Put	Split	Throw	Whirl
Call	Draw	Have	Make	Run	Stand	Tie	Work

How to Use the Right "Trigger" Words

"Trigger words are specific words that can be used to rouse a person's emotions immediately," says Nancy Cooper, a copywriter for a San Diego television station. "Scientific experiments conducted with the polygraph show that certain words cause a definite reaction in most people.

"Television and radio advertisers invest millions and millions of dollars in commercials. Most of these commercials are only 30 seconds long so each of those expensive ticks of the clock must be crammed full of persuasion. Here is a list of 21 of the most persuasive and compelling words those scientific experiments have shown us to use in our advertising:

Amazing	Guarantee	Listen	Money	Power	Results	See
Discovery	Health	Look	New	Proud	Safety	Watch
Easy	Important	Love	Now	Proven	Save	You

"Every word must count for something, and any message that doesn't use as many of these words as possible will have very little appeal to the listener. Choosing the right trigger word for a commercial is one of the copywriter's biggest jobs."

How to Get Rid of the Deadwood in Your Vocabulary

Deadwood consists of particles, prepositions, prepositional phrases, conjunctions, and so on, that add little meaning to your sentence, and can often confuse or muddle your meaning.

Since they make up more than half of all the words you use, it makes a great deal of difference whether they are simple and concise —for instance, *so, for, if, since, because*—or long and complicated, such as *accordingly, for the purpose of, in the event that, due to the fact that, inasmuch as, for the reason that.*

To rid your vocabulary of this deadwood, always follow the rule that one "dead" word is better than two or three dead ones, and a short dead word is better than a long one. If you can get rid of the dead word altogether, so much the better, of course.

Here is the list of deadwood I try to avoid. Instead of using the dead words in this list, use the ones in parentheses instead. You will be amazed how clean and clear your writing and speaking will become by just doing this alone.

Accordingly   (so)
Afford an opportunity   (permit, let)
Along the lines of   (like)
As to   (about)
At all times   (always)
At an early date   (soon)
At the present time   (now)
At your earliest convenience   (as soon as you can)
Consequently   (so)
Due to the fact that   (since, because)
For the purpose of   (for)
For the reason that   (since, because)
For this reason   (so)
From the point of view of   (for)
Furthermore   (then)
Hence   (so)
In accordance with   (by, under)
In addition to   (besides, also)
In compliance with your request   (as you asked)
In favor of   (for, to)

In order to   (to)
In the amount of   (for)
In the case of   (if)
In the event that   (if)
In the near future   (soon)
In the nature of   (like)
In terms of   (in, for)
In the neighborhood of   (about)
In view of the fact that   (as)
Inasmuch as   (since, because)
Incidentally   (by the way)
Indeed   (in fact)
Likewise   (and, also)
More specifically   (for instance, for example)
Moreover   (now, next)
Nevertheless   (but, however)
On the basis of   (by)
On the grounds that   (since, because)
Prior to   (before)
That is to say   (in other words)
Thus   (so)
To be sure   (of course)
With a view to   (to)
With reference to   (about)
With regard to   (about)
With the result that   (so that)

Use These Simple Yet Powerful Words;
They're Guaranteed to Work

Many years ago when I was in the army, I was awarded the Army Commendation Medal. When I read the citation that went along with the decoration, I could hardly understand the flamboyant and flowery terms that had been used to describe what I'd done.

My youngest son, Larry, read the citation, too, and said, "I don't understand what they said or exactly what you did, Dad, but *I'm sure proud of you!*" And I thought to myself, *Gee, he said it better in those five short words than the army had in five hundred.*

You see, you don't need a lot of big flowery words and phrases to put miracle people power to work for you. Little words like my son used will do just fine.

Here, then, are some of the most powerful words and phrases you can ever use to get the results you want. Paste them in your hat and use them. I guarantee they'll work for you.

I'm proud of you.
What is your opinion?
You did a good job.
I need your help.
We can't do it without you.
It's all my fault.
I made a mistake.
I'm sorry.
If you please.
Thanks a lot.
You.

How to Add New Words to Your Vocabulary Every Day

Lots of people use the dictionary to look up big words to add to their vocabulary. I do just the opposite. I look up a big word to find out how I can use a small word in its place so I'll never have to use that big word again.

For instance, the other day I read the word "dichotomization" in an article on religion. I looked the word up and found out that it meant the process of dividing something into two parts. Now I know how to use the word, but I never will.

Instead of using it as the author did when he spoke of the "dichotomization of the church," I'll simply say, "the church split into two branches," or "the church split into two parts," and everyone will know exactly what I mean. No one will ever have to wonder what I said.

If you want to streamline your own word arsenal to make it more powerful and effective, then use your dictionary the same way I do: to make little ones out of big ones. I know you'll be most happy with the end results.

In a Nutshell

I can think of no better way to sum up this chapter on how to double and triple your miracle people power with the words you use than to quote this article by Joseph A. Ecclesine from *Printers' Ink* Magazine. I only wish that I had written it.

BIG WORDS ARE FOR THE BIRDS [1]

When you come right down to it, there is no law that says you *have* to use big words when you write or talk.

There are lots of small words, and good ones, that can be made to say all the things you want to say, quite as well as the big ones. It may take a bit more time to find them at first. But it can be well worth it, for all of us know what they mean. Some small words, more than you might think, are rich with just the right feel, the right taste, as if made to help you say a thing the way it should be said.

Small words can be crisp, brief, terse—go to the point, like a knife. They have a charm all their own. They dance, twist, turn, sing. Like sparks in the night they light the way for the eyes of those who read. They are the grace notes of prose. You know what they say the way you know a day is bright and fair—at first sight. And you find, as you read, that you like the way they say it. Small words are gay. And they can catch large thoughts and hold them up for all to see, like rare stones in rings of gold, or joy in the eyes of a child. Some make you feel, as well as see: the cold deep dark of night, the hot salt sting of tears.

Small words move with ease where big words stand still—or, worse, bog down and get in the way of what you want to say. There is not much, in all truth, that small words will not say—and say quite well.

---

[1] Joseph A. Ecclesine, *"Big Words Are for the Birds,"* Printers' Ink Publishing Company, Inc., New York, 1961.

8

How to Put Miracle People Power into Everything You Say

I want to show you how to put miracle people power into everything you say so you can get the results that you're after. That is extremely important to you, for studies made at the University of Michigan show that the average person spends approximately 85 percent of his time in oral communication.

When people listen to you and understand you—when they really get your message—when you put miracle people power into everything you say—you'll be able to achieve your purpose in speaking with them. They'll do as you want them to do.

For instance, if you're a salesman . . . people will buy. If you're a foreman or supervisor . . . your subordinates will do the job properly for you. If you're an executive, a manager, an employer, a teacher . . . they'll carry out your orders or your instructions. And if you're a father or mother . . . your children will do as you ask them to do.

So you see, no matter what kind of job you have or what sort of work you do, what you say and how you say it will determine to a great extent just how successful you are in influencing people so you can get them to do as you desire.

Now of course I don't know what you do for a living, but I'm sure that you use hundreds and thousands of words every day in your conversations with your friends, neighbors, and family . . . your boss, your employees, fellow workers, salesmen, customers, and so on.

Some of this conversation may be just small talk, but I will bet that most of your verbal effort is directed, even though perhaps often haphazardly, at getting people to see things your way and to do things your way.

Now just imagine for a moment how much more it would help your prospects of success if all your talk and conversation were consciously directed toward achieving miracle power with people, so you could attain your specific objectives and reach your individual goals. Think of all the good things that will be yours when you are able to put miracle people power into everything you say. Just for instance, I know that—

YOU'LL GAIN THESE BENEFITS

1. *You'll increase your powers of persuasion.* People will do as you want them to do.

2. *People will cooperate with you* when you put your message across to them clearly and concisely.

3. *There'll be a genuine meeting of the minds* when you use miracle people power to gain clear communication.

4. *You'll achieve your purposes.* Goals can be reached, missions accomplished, objectives attained.

5. *You'll succeed,* for it's a proven fact that successful people know how to communicate their desires clearly and succinctly to others.

TECHNIQUES YOU CAN USE TO GAIN THESE BENEFITS

How to Develop Your Own Style

The person who is able to put miracle people power into everything he says is always his own natural self. He does not try to show off his knowledge or his superiority. He will act and talk as a friendly and likeable human being who has a mind always open to new ideas.

Such a person will not be artificial. He will not copy others nor will he use an affected accent. He will not pretend to be what he is not. This kind of man or woman will be warmly appreciated and welcomed by everyone everywhere.

Will Rogers was this kind of person. He was an Oklahoma cowboy first, last, and always. And no matter where he spoke or entertained —New York, Chicago, San Francisco—people loved him for just being himself. Will Rogers never once pretended to be someone that he wasn't or couldn't be. But he could really put miracle people power into everything he said, and that's for sure.

So if you want to put this same miracle people power into everything you say, too, then be yourself. I don't mean you shouldn't try to improve your speaking abilities; you should. But don't become artificial or phony or insincere in the process. The best way to make a favorable lasting impression on people is to be yourself and use your own natural speaking voice. Don't be a copycat or try to imitate anybody. This idea of being honest and sincere leads me quite naturally to my next point, which is:

Don't Try to Sell People an Empty Box

In his book, *How to Sell Yourself to Others,*[1] Elmer Wheeler discusses his four famous "Wheelerpoints" for selling yourself to others, the second one of which is *don't sell an empty box.*

> Mr. Wheeler says, "You will find many Tested Methods, many Tested 'Selling' Words, and Tested Techniques, used by successful and famous people to put themselves across and to attain success.
> "But the biggest *success secret* of all is *sincerity.*
> "Without sincerity none of the methods herein given will work for you. Sincerity is the magic touchstone that makes you sizzle instead of fizzle."

How true. If you're not honest and sincere with people, you'll get nowhere at all. Oh, you might make a little progress for a little while, for after all, it is a proven fact that you can fool some of the people part of the time, but if you're a phony, if you're not really honest and sincere, you'll not have enough staying power for the long haul. Sooner or later people will discover that you're as counterfeit as a three dollar bill.

---

[1] Elmer Wheeler, *How to Sell Yourself to Others* (Prentice-Hall, Inc., Englewood Cliffs, New Jersey, 1947).

So if you do want to succeed, if you do want to put miracle people power into everything you say, then be honest and sincere with people. As Elmer Wheeler puts it, "Don't try to sell people an empty box. Put something in it first."

Use This Magic Formula: People Will Always Listen to You

The words of Charles M. Schwab, Andrew Carnegie's million dollar a year troubleshooter, are practically immortal. He said in effect, "The way to develop the best that is in a man is by appreciation and encouragement. There is nothing that will so kill the ambitions of a man as criticism from his superiors. I never criticize anyone. I am always anxious to praise, but I am reluctant to find fault. When I like anything, I am hearty in my approbation and lavish in my praise."

I, too, know of nothing that will stimulate a person more than sincere praise and appreciation. If you want to put miracle people power into everything you say, then tell the other person how good he is, how much you think of him, what a fine job he's done. If you can't compliment him for the good work he's done, then tell him you know what a good job he's going to do in the future for you.

Now I am not alone in my feeling that praise and miracle people power go together. Down through the years, many people have felt that praise and appreciation do have a kind of miracle working power on people.

One prominent individual who felt that way was Charles Fillmore, co-founder of the Unity School of Christianity near Kansas City, Missouri. He said this: "Words of praise, gratitude, or thanksgiving expand, set free, and in every way radiate energy. You can praise a weak body into strength; a fearful heart into peace and trust; shattered nerves into poise and power; a failing business into prosperity and success; want and insufficiency into supply and support."

I have never seen a more dramatic and striking example of how praise and appreciation can bring out the best that is in a person than when I witnessed a hotel fire in Des Moines, Iowa, many, many years ago.

A fireman was working his way slowly and cautiously up the

ladder to the third floor where a young girl stood in a window. Suddenly there was an explosion on the second floor. Flames and smoke billowed out of the windows and the ladder swayed. The fireman hesitated and took a couple of steps downward.

Then someone in the crowd below began to clap his hands. Others joined in. Soon everyone was applauding and yelling encouragement to the fireman. And he, spurred on by their praise and appreciation for his brave efforts, went back up the ladder to rescue the young girl.

How You Can Put This Technique to Work for Yourself

Perhaps you think it's difficult to compliment a person and be really sincere about it, especially in the average, ordinary, and routine events of a day. That's not true at all. It's easy. It just takes a little effort and a bit of forethought. You can praise a person for what he *does,* not what he *is,* like this:

RIGHT: Jack, you win the award for most sales this month.
WRONG: Jack, you're the best salesman in our company.

RIGHT: Sally, you did an excellent job on this letter.
WRONG: Sally, you're the finest typist in our secretarial pool.

RIGHT: Henry, you did an outstanding piece of work on that last project you handled.
WRONG: Henry, you're the best production employee in our whole plant.

You see, when you praise a person for *what* he does, you have to be specific about it. That in turn forces you to be sincere. But if you praise an individual for what he *is,* your compliment can easily turn into nothing but pure flattery. Then it will sound phony and insincere.

Not only that, praising the act rather than the person avoids embarrassment, for most people feel uncomfortable if you compliment them for what they are. But when you pick out something specific the person has done that you can praise, then he feels good, about it.

And no doubt about it, we all like to be praised. As Mark Twain once said, "I can live for two months on a good compliment."

What to Do if You're Asked to Give a Speech or Talk

I am not going to attempt in this book to make you into a professional public speaker. If that were your purpose, I'm sure you would be reading a specific book on that subject.

But I do know, if you're like most of us, there will be times when you do want to speak up before a large group of people. And if you can talk effectively, people will notice you and remember you.

Just for instance, when's the last time you wanted to stand up and speak your mind in your Sunday School class, but you didn't because you were afraid or you didn't feel properly prepared? Or what about the times you've wanted to express your opinions at a PTA meeting, present your viewpoint to the town council, or address a convention meeting—yet you didn't because you didn't feel qualified?

This short section will help you overcome those obstacles so you can become a more confident and effective speaker. Here are the steps you can take to do that:

Get Your Material Together

Unless this is strictly an impromptu talk made on only a moment's notice, you should gather together the material you need to make your talk. No doubt you'll need to do some reading and note-taking to bring yourself completely up-to-date on your subject.

Make Up Your Outline

After you've gathered your material, it's time to organize it. If you don't organize your notes, you could sound like the speaker I heard once at a convention in Miami. He rambled and wandered for ten minutes or so without coming to any point whatever. His audience grew nervous and restless. Sensing this, he stopped and said, "Please be patient with me. When I get through talking here, I'm going to say something." Only his sense of humor saved his speech from being a total failure. You might not be so lucky.

The best way to organize your material is to make up an outline. There may be many other ways to make up an outline for your talk, but in my own experience, I've found the following one to be extremely useful to me.

1. The opening.
2. Benefits to be gained.
3. Techniques to be used.
4. Examples of others who've succeeded by using these techniques.
5. Conclusion.

1. **The Opening** sets the theme of your talk. It is used to gain the immediate attention of your listeners. You can use any of the following methods to do that:

a) A startling statement of fact.
b) An unusual anecdote.
c) A strong example.
d) An authoritative quotation.
e) An arresting question.

2. **The Benefits to Be Gained** are stressed to keep your listeners interested and to show them how your talk will be helpful to them.

3. **Techniques to Be Used.** Tell your listeners how they can gain the benefits you've offered or told them about.

4. **Examples of Others Who've Succeeded** should be given to prove that the techniques you've offered really do work. They must be relative to your topic or the theme of your subject. To lend them authenticity, you should be specific about names, occupations, dates, and places.

5. **Your Conclusion** can be either an appeal for action of some sort or a summary of your talk. This will depend primarily on whether your talk is made to persuade or inform your listeners.

Practice Your Talk

After you've made all your preparations, then practice your talk in front of a mirror or on your family to work out the bugs and to get rid of any nervousness you might have. Don't memorize your talk word for word, except for perhaps one or two sentences in your opening and your conclusion. It's all right to use a few notes on 3 by 5 cards to keep track of where you are, but you should *never read your talk*.

As I say, this short section will not turn you into a professional public speaker or a platform lecturer, but it will help you sharpen your speaking skills so you can put miracle people power into everything you say, and that, after all, is what you're really after.

Ten Tips That Will Help You Put Miracle People Power into Everything You Say

1. **Speak with the Voice of Authority.** To be able to do this, you must really know your stuff. The more you know about your subject, the better off you'll be when you're talking with people.

2. **Use Simple Words and Short Sentences.** It's the simple things that last longest and wear best. The simplest writing is always the best because it's easiest to understand. The same can be said about speeches and conversation.

3. **Use Concrete and Specific Words and Phrases.** The absolute master of this art was Jesus Christ. The words he used and the order He gave were simple, concise, to the point, and easy to understand when He said, "Follow me."

4. **Avoid Needless Words and Useless Information.** The person who talks much usually says very little. Don't clutter up your listener's mind with unimportant trivia and worthless details. As my minister puts it, "Most preachers say more than they have to talk

about. I'd rather quit before I'm through than run the risk of boring people." Smart man. No wonder his church is always full.

5. **Be Direct and to the Point.** This idea is fundamental to achieving miracle people power in everything you say. If you concentrate on a single point, you'll not scatter your fire. You'll be able to zero in on your target.

6. **Don't Exaggerate.** Not only should you never exaggerate or stretch the truth, but you would also be wise to understate your case. Then you need have no fear of any repercussions.

7. **Don't Talk Down to Your Listeners.** Even though you might be the authority on your subject, that's still no reason for you to talk down to your listeners or to lord it over them. I've never yet met a person who wasn't more knowledgeable than I was in some area.

8. **Be Diplomatic and Tactful.** Tact is the ability to say the right thing at just the right place and the right time without offending anyone. You especially need to be tactful and diplomatic when you're dealing with difficult persons or touchy situations. An easy way to be tactful and diplomatic with everyone is to treat every man like a gentleman and every woman like a lady.

9. **Present the Proposition That Is Best for Your Listener,** not the one that is best for you. Do this and no one will ever be able to cut the ground out from under you. Your defenses will be impenetrable.

10. **Answer All Questions Frankly and Openly.** If you've followed the guidance I gave you in the first nine tips, you'll have no trouble at all with this one.

9

How to Write Letters That Are Loaded with Miracle People Power

One of the best ways to increase your miracle people power is to write clear and concise, strong and forceful letters, memorandums, and reports. It doesn't matter who or what you are—preacher, salesman, politician, supervisor, manager, teacher, executive, businessman—if you can make yourself easily understood in your writing, you'll increase tremendously your chances of becoming successful.

A great many times you'll have to use letters and directives to get people to do as you want them to do. Perhaps you won't be able to contact people face-to-face, or you'll need to follow up with a letter to get them to do as you desire. So it's important to you that you be able to handle yourself well on paper because *people who can command words to serve their thoughts and feelings will be able to command others to serve their purposes.*

Let me ask you this now: Are your letters and reports vague, nonspecific, abstract, and hard to decode? Does what you say on paper cause other people to make mistakes? Or worse yet, does it irritate your readers and make enemies for you? Does it cause you to lose customers, antagonize new prospects, and miss out on sales? Do you ever find yourself writing another letter or sending in a second report to clear up what you said in the first one? Do you ever write a letter, sign it, put it in the envelope, seal and stamp it, only to tear the envelope open to read it again because you're not sure your meaning is clear? Do you ever get phone calls asking you to explain exactly what you meant in your letter or your report?

If any of these things have ever happened to you, or if you're not satisfied with your present writing abilities for any reason whatever, then the techniques here in Chapter 9 are just right for you. They won't turn you into a professional writer by any means, but they will help you make your writing clear, concise, to the point, and easy to understand. They'll help you streamline your correspondence so you can say what you really want to say. Besides that,

YOU'LL ALSO GAIN THESE BENEFITS

You'll Better Your Chances of Getting Ahead

If you work for a company or a big corporation, you'll better your chances to get ahead if you can handle yourself well on paper. Learn to write with clarity and force, make what you write simple and easy to understand, and you'll attract the attention of the brass up topside where it really counts. Then, without a doubt, you'll be promoted far ahead of the person who cannot express himself clearly and concisely in writing.

You'll Be Able to Put Yourself Across to Others

Every letter you write and every report you make is a personal contact, or it should be, with another person. To many people who have never seen you—your letters and reports represent you. They tell your reader what kind of person you are. So express yourself clearly, make what you say easy to understand, and you'll be able to put yourself across to your reader.

You'll Increase Your Miracle People Power with Good Writing

Write your letters so that people will gladly do what you want them to do, and you'll increase your miracle people power. Why is it so important for you to write with clarity and force? Well, as I said in the first part of this chapter, people who can command words to serve their thoughts and feelings will be able to command others to serve their purposes. And that's miracle people power in a nutshell.

TECHNIQUES YOU CAN USE TO GAIN THESE BENEFITS

The Six Basic Steps of Effective Letter Writing

First off, I'd like you to get the mechanics of effective letter writing down pat. Once you have the basic steps firmly in mind, then I can show you how to arouse your reader's interest, how to get him to take action, how to put a "hook" in your letters, the format you can use for a persuasive letter, and some specific miracle people power guidelines to use in your letter writing. But first things first.

1. Know *Why* You're Writing Your Letter

If you know your purpose in writing your letter, if the objective to be gained is clear in your mind, then your writing will also be clear. However, if your objective is vague and abstract, then your writing will also be vague and abstract. So before you start your letter, know *why* you're writing it. Determine exactly what it is that you want to gain.

Letters normally fall into three general categories: (1) *to order or direct,* (2) *to inform,* (3) *to persuade.* All three are concerned with *who, what, when, where, why,* and *how,* but the emphasis will be different in each case depending on your purpose.

For instance, a letter that directs action indicates *what* has to be done. An informative letter will usually tell a person *how* to do something. A persuasive letter is written to explain *why* a certain action ought to be taken.

Of course, these purposes often overlap, as when you make a directive or an order more understandable or more palatable by explaining the *how* and *why* as well as the *what.* Or if you were writing a persuasive letter to your boss asking him to approve the use of some new equipment, you would emphasize *why* it should be used, but you would no doubt also explain *how* it would work.

So even though you might have some overlapping in your letters, keeping these three basic categories in mind will help you find clear explanations or convincing reasons to back up the specific objectives that you're after.

2. Know Your Reader

Who is going to read your letter? A person with a **PHD** behind his name or a man with an eighth grade education? You'll be able to get your point across only when you use words and ideas your reader can easily understand. Whether a person reads you loud and clear depends on *his* training, knowledge, and experience—not on yours.

If you're writing a letter to go on a bulletin board for all factory employees to read, you must write so clearly that the least educated person in the plant can understand what you've said.

"A lot of directives here at the plant are written at college levels of readability and understanding," says Harry Fisher, vice president of DeWitt-Newton, Inc., manufacturers of industrial and commercial metal buildings. "The writer forgets that men of modest education— our production employees—must read them and act on them. I do my best to get everyone to keep their letters simple enough for everyone to understand."

It is important for you to determine who your reader is going to be, too. Always ask yourself, "Who must read and understand this letter?" The answer should influence the words as well as the ideas that you use.

3. Lay the Proper Foundation

Effective letter writing is based on proper preparation—the selection, analysis, and organization of your ideas. Your preparation may take only a few minutes or perhaps several days. It will all depend on the size of your problem. But either way it will be one of the most important parts of your letter writing efforts.

"Many people write useless and ineffective letters because they start writing them before they're actually ready to begin," says Margaret Eaton, an instructor in business correspondence and effective letter writing at Mid-America Business College in Cedar Rapids, Iowa. "That's why their letters aren't satisfactory and don't produce the desired results they want."

I agree wholeheartedy with Margaret. Before you pick up a pen or sit down at your typewriter, think your problem through before writing about it. Get the answers to *who, what, when, where, why,* and *how* first. Then it's time to sit down at your desk and start the actual job of writing.

4. Identify and Pinpoint Your Main Ideas

"Successful writers know that deciding what to leave out is just as important as what to leave in," says Frank Gammon. Frank, who writes articles for trade journals, also teaches a class in creative writing in Drury College's Adult Education Division two nights a week in Springfield, Missouri.

"Words, ideas, and facts that are not essential to the understanding or the acceptance of your specific objective can only hide and weaken it.

"It doesn't really matter whether your writing is based on your personal knowledge, reading and research, or both. The problem you face is usually too much material rather than not enough.

"So preparing to write is primarily a process of defining, sifting, and discarding until you have left only one clear purpose or objective in mind and the main ideas necessary either to support it or reach it."

I can vouch for the truth of what Frank says. I find that in writing a book, my biggest problem is not what to say, but what *not* to say.

5. Write from an Outline

Any piece of writing—be it a book, an article, or a letter—can be done more logically and quickly from an outline. If you're writing a long several page letter, you may need to work from a written outline. If it's a short letter, a simple outline in your head may be all that you need.

An outline makes your writing plan easy to see and helps you keep your specific objective clearly in mind. But it is worthless unless you stick to it and work from it. This is not to say that you should not change your outline here and there if some better ideas occur to you. You should. In this respect, your outline should be a working sketch —not a final blueprint.

But on the other hand, you should not let your outline get so far out of hand that it develops a case of elephantiasis. This can come from a loss of control in sticking to your original outline.

6. Review Your Letter for Objectivity

Unless you're writing a chatty personal family letter or a love letter to your sweetheart, chances are you won't have a finished product ready to go on the first attempt. When you've completed your first draft, you should review and revise your work.

The better you become in your letter writing, the fewer drafts you'll have to make, but I doubt if you'll ever reach the point where one is enough. Perhaps you will; I never have.

In my own case, I'm down to four drafts when I write professionally for publication—two longhand and two typewritten—but I doubt seriously if I'll ever be able to get below that number.

Since most people write more letters to persuade than to inform or direct, I want to spend the rest of this chapter showing you how to *sell* yourself to your reader, or how to *slant* your letter so your reader will want to do what you want him to do.

How to Arouse Your Reader's Interest in What You Write

"When you sit down to write a letter to persuade a person to do as you want him to do, you must not think of what you want from him," says Alberta Harris, owner of the Royal Collection Service in Phoenix, Arizona. "Even if you're a bill collector like I am, you must always think in terms of what your reader wants first.

"I know, for instance, that most people want to have a good credit rating. So it's up to me to convince the person that his credit rating is more important to him than not paying the bill."

The reader of your letter wants certain things out of life, too. If you will remember, I told you back in the first chapter about the 12 basic needs and desires each normal person has. Rather than repeat them all here, let me just nutshell them for you like this:

Every normal person wants to know how to be loved—how to win fame, fortune, power—and how to stay healthy.

Now you must keep in mind what your reader wants when you write your letter to get him to do something for you. You must show him how doing what you want will bring him a step closer to his own goals.

It doesn't matter at all whether you're trying to sell your reader a pair of shoes, making a proposal of marriage, or attempting to collect a debt. In each case, you're trying to persuade your reader to do something for you. He will do it only if the doing of it brings him nearer his own goal, or if the fear of not doing it will remove that goal farther away from him.

So you see, it is essential that you know what your reader wants. Even if he's a complete stranger to you, you know what his main interests are for all of us have the same basic needs and desires.

Instead of rushing in to tell him about your goals, your interests, your needs, and your desires, make your point of contact with him his goals, his interests, his needs, and his desires. That's the only way you can be sure of gaining his attention and holding his interest.

How to Get Your Reader to Take Action

To get your reader to take action and do what you want him to do, you must appeal to one of those basic prime movers we've already talked about. Sometimes those basic needs and desires are so mixed together it's hard to tell which one to work on the most.

The more motives you can appeal to, the more chances you'll have for success. However, it is important that you distinguish between a motive that makes a person merely *want* to do something, and the motive that *compels* him to take the action you desire. Here's what Loretta Ingram, owner of the Village Fashion Shoppe in Hot Springs, Arkansas, says about that.

> "Your reader may not *want* to pay you a bill she owes," Loretta says. "She may *want* to keep the money for herself right now and pay you later on. Your job is to *sell* her on the idea that her credit is more important to her than her temporary possession of the money or whatever it will buy. Convince her of that and you'll have touched the right motive; she'll take the action you want her to take. You can also add some incentive by reminding her how important it will be to have good credit with you when the new fall or spring fashions come out."

Getting your reader to take action, then, comes down to making him want to do what you want him to do more than what he wants to do. When you can get him thinking and moving along those lines, when you can bring home to him the benefits he'll gain by doing what you want him to do in such a way that he will want those benefits more than anything else, you'll have put miracle people power into your letters. He'll take the action you want him to take; he'll do the things you want him to do.

How to Put a "Hook" into Your Letters

No letter is complete without the close, and no close is complete without the "hook." You may have written a wonderfully persuasive letter. Could be you've aroused your reader's attention, captured his interest, and sparked his desire, but if you don't "hook" him, he may not take the action you want him to take.

Your reader will do what you want him to do for one of two reasons. The first is that you've made him so anxious to get what you've offered that he'll take the required action immediately. But most people tend to procrastinate. They want to think it over so they put things off for a while. So you must give him another reason to take action, and that's where the hook comes in.

You must make this kind of reader realize how he's going to lose out if he doesn't immediately do as you ask him to do. The hook provides a penalty if your reader fails to take action. That is the second reason the reader will do as you ask. And unless your hook arouses fear in your reader that he will lose something worthwhile if he does not act at once, you won't get the results that you want.

Remember that fear is on the opposite side of the coin of desire. If you can't move a person to action by arousing his desire, then turn the coin over and move him to action by arousing his fear.

"When you use fear to get what you want, you must be specific and definite," says Phil Jackson, owner of the True Value Hardware Store in Ames, Iowa. "If you're threatening a person with a lawsuit for not paying you what he owes, tell him the exact date his account will go to your lawyer. And tell him who your lawyer is—complete with address and telephone number.

"Or if you're going to raise your prices and you want to get all the orders you can before you do, specify the exact date your prices will go up. Or if you have only a few articles left, indicate the exact quantity that is available, and let your reader know that it's strictly 'first come—first served,' period."

A successful close to your letter has two parts, then. One part tells the reader what to do and how to do it. It reiterates the benefits to be gained and uses persuasion and inducement to get the job done. The second part of the close tells the person what will happen to him or what he will lose if he doesn't take the necessary action. This is the "hook" that catches the reluctant reader and impels him to take the action you want him to take.

Use This Format for a Persuasive Letter

If you're trying to use your miracle people power to persuade your reader to take action, here is a format you can use. I have found it to be highly successful for me.

1. *The Opening.* Here you grab your reader's attention immediately by fitting in with his train of thought (his basic human needs and desires). You establish your point of contact with his self-interests to excite and arouse his curiosity so he will read further into your letter.

2. *You Cover the Benefits to Be Gained.* As soon as you have your reader's attention, tell him how he's going to benefit by doing as you ask. Give him a reason or a motive to take action. Do this, not merely by describing what your product or your proposal is, but by letting him know what it will do for him. Tell him about the profit, the pleasure, the convenience, and so on that he will gain.

3. *Offer Proof of What You Say.* The best proof you can offer that your proposition will give him the benefits you've listed is to tell him of others who've benefited, too. Let him check with Sam Jones, Sally Brown, or Joe Grey so he can find out for himself that you're telling him the truth.

4. *Tell Him How He Can Gain Those Benefits.* You usually do this in the next to last paragraph of your letter. Here you give your reader his exact instructions. You tell him exactly what he must do to gain the benefits you've offered him.

5. *Close with the Hook*. This is the snapper or the penalty you hold over your reluctant reader's head. You hook him and force him to take action by telling him about the loss in money or prestige or opportunity that will be his if he does not act at once. You normally place the hook in the last paragraph of your letter.

How to Use These Nine Miracle People Power Guidelines in Your Writing

1. **Write the Same Way You Talk.** Many people do not write the same way they talk. They use pompous words and stilted phrases that they never would use in a conversation in an effort to impress their reader.

The best way to avoid this unnatural style of writing is simply to write the same way you talk. If people understand you when you talk, then they'll also understand you when you *talk on paper*. After all, that should be your main purpose—to be understood—not to dazzle or impress your reader with your knowledge and education.

2. **How to Make Your Meaning Clear.** Clear writing is easy to understand. It is concise and concrete, direct and to the point. To make your own writing clear, use simple one and two syllable words and present your ideas one at a time.

Even the most technical explanation can be understood if you surround your technical terms with simple words and give your reader a new sentence for each new idea. Too many connectives make for complex and compound sentences that confuse and bewilder your reader. You lose him too easily. When you come to the end of one idea, stop your thought with a period. Then begin a new sentence.

3. **How to Give Your Writing Force.** Simple one-syllable verbs like *run, work, make, do,* and so on give your writing force. Verbs bring strength and vigor to your writing. They create movement and make things happen.

If you want to make your writing forceful, simply say who *does* or who *did* what. Any sentence that does not tell who does or who did what is a weak sentence.

4. **Use the Active Voice of the Verb.** As long as you say who does or who did what, your sentence will be forceful and strong. You'll use the active voice of the verb. The moment you say *what was done by whom,* you've switched to the passive voice. Your sentence has become weak and colorless.

The clue to watch for is the preposition *by.* You can see the difference in the following pairs of right and wrong sentences.

RIGHT: The council approved the report.
WRONG: The report was approved *by* the council.

RIGHT: Sally typed this letter.
WRONG: This letter was typed *by* Sally.

RIGHT: I mailed your check this afternoon.
WRONG: Your check was mailed this afternoon *by* me.

5. **Use Your Own Language.** Forget business English. Use the same words you would use in your home or talking over the fence to your neighbor. If you use *such* terms as *okay, no sweat, good deal, horse of a different color* when you talk, then do the same when you write. Use colloquial English whenever you want to. It's a good way to keep from writing formal and pompous letters.

6. **Don't Be Old-Fashioned.** I'm sure when you talk you don't use such phrases as *your favor has come to hand, acknowledge receipt of, yours with regard to the above,* and the like. Is that really the way you talk? I doubt it. So *for heaven's sake,* don't write that way.

7. **Use Contractions.** It's perfectly all right to use *don't, won't, can't, couldn't, wouldn't,* and so forth in your writing. To tell the truth, it's almost impossible to write pompous and stuffy letters when you use contractions. Besides, using contractions is one of the best ways of insuring that you'll write as you talk.

8. **Don't Worry About Grammar.** You do not need to be a grammarian to write a good clear sentence. After all, the first requirement of grammar is that you focus your attention on the meaning you want your reader to get. If you take care to make your meaning clear, your grammar will usually take care of itself.

9. **Be Yourself** . . . **Not Someone Else.** Don't try to be someone you're not when you write a letter. So many of us try to impress our readers with our self-importance or our status and we fail miserably. Let your own personality shine through in your writing. The best way you can do that is to write with the words you normally use every day of your life.

10

How You Can Control the Actions and Attitudes of Complete Strangers with Miracle People Power

To make a good first impression is more than half the job of achieving miracle people power with total strangers. The way you strike people at your first meeting will usually decide how they're going to react to you for a long time to come.

If you rub a person the wrong way the first time you meet him, it could take months or even years to correct his initial bad impression of you. Your first few words are more important than your next several thousand.

Just for instance, now, suppose you've got a mean "I-hate-the-whole-world-look" on your face the first time you meet a person. No matter how many times you see him after that, he'll always remember that first bad impression he had of you. He'll continually think of you as an old sourpuss with a miserable outlook on life.

For example, the other day I was talking with Scott Kennedy at a Kiwanis luncheon. Another person, a local businessman—let's just call him John—joined us in small talk for a few minutes.

After he left, Scott said, "I can't stand that man. He's got a filthy rotten temper. Treats his help horribly."

I was astonished at Scott's remark and I said, "I don't understand that at all, Scott. I've known John for a long time. He's one of the most pleasant, best-natured fellows in the whole town. I've never seen him lose his temper in all the time I've known him."

"Well, all I know is I went into his store one time," Scott said, "and he was chewing out one of his clerks up by the cash register. He was really raising Cain. He was all redfaced and yelling like crazy."

"I'm really surprised to hear that," I said. "It sure isn't like him at all. Something really bad must have happened to cause John to act that way that one time. I know it had to be the exception for he's one of the most even-tempered men I've ever known."

"Maybe so," Scott said. "But I've never gone back in his place again and I'm not going to. I have absolutely no use for businessmen who use their position to mistreat their employees that way."

Actually, I happen to know that John is one of the most patient, kind, and thoughtful employers I've ever seen. He goes out of his way to be decent to his help. I also know that he has made several loans without interest to some of his employees' children to help them through college. But unfortunately, he lost his temper that one time Scott saw him. And Scott's first impression of John was a lasting one.

So it's highly important for you to know how to make the right impression on people the first time out. I want to use this chapter to show you how you can get off on the right foot with strangers so you can influence their actions and attitudes from the very beginning. When you know how to do that,

YOU'LL GAIN THESE IMPORTANT BENEFITS

1. When you use the first technique in Chapter 10, people will not only become interested in you, but they'll also like you at once.

2. Use the second technique and complete strangers will go out of their way to help you.

3. The third technique will enable you to make friends instantly with a total stranger whom you've never met before.

4. You'll learn how to get what you want from others by controlling their emotions and attitudes in the fourth technique.

5. You'll be able to control the actions of strangers when you use the infallible methods shown in the fifth technique.

TECHNIQUES YOU CAN USE TO GAIN THESE BENEFITS

Use This Technique; Everyone Will Like You Immediately

Professor William James once said, "The deepest principle in human nature is the craving to be appreciated." You can fulfill that deep craving in a complete stranger with something that doesn't cost you a single cent: *an unexpected compliment.*

Compliment a person and you'll be amazed at the preferential treatment you'll receive. I could give you a list of examples here as long as my arm where I personally have received better than average service as a result of my saying something kind to a complete stranger. Let me tell you briefly about just two of them:

The Waitress in the Busy Restaurant. It was Saturday night and the place was jammed with the weekend crowd. My wife and I were due at a meeting at eight o'clock. We had to be on time for I was the main speaker. So we decided to sit at the counter for faster service, rather than wait for a booth or a table.

Our waitress, nervous and worn-out, poured our coffee and said irritably, "I hope you're not in a hurry. It'll be at least 20 minutes before I can even turn your order in. The kitchen just can't handle any more for a while."

I looked at her name tag on her left breast pocket and said, "April Dawn. What a delightful name. It sounds so gay and sparkling and carefree. I don't think I've ever heard it before. I'm sure you must be happy every day that your parents gave you such a lovely name."

"Thank you for being so nice," she said, suddenly smiling and taking her order pad from her pocket. "Most people just call me *waitress* or *hey you!* Let me take your order right now, and I'll sneak it into the kitchen ahead of the others."

"I'd sure appreciate it if you could," I said. "To tell you the truth, I don't think I can afford to wait 20 minutes. I have an important meeting in just a little over an hour that I dare not miss."

"You won't miss it," she said. "I'll tell the chef your problem so he can take care of you right away. I guarantee you'll make your meeting on time." And we did.

The Desk Clerk in the Motel. My wife and I had stopped in an extremely tasteful motel called *Holiday West* in Elk City, a small town in western Oklahoma on our way to Los Angeles. The room had been an outstanding bargain. It had a kingsize bed that just fit the bill at the end of a hard day's drive. I made a mental note of the room number and vowed if we came that way again to stay in the same one.

It was nearly two years later when we had the opportunity to stay there again. But we had to drive an extra two hours that day to reach Elk City. By the time we got there we were both exhausted. Although I remembered the room number, I'd forgotten the name of the motel, so we'd been unable to call ahead to reserve that specific room.

"We stayed here two years ago," I told the lady at the desk. "You probably don't remember me, but I remember you well. You gave us room number six. It was absolutely wonderful. We liked it so well and enjoyed that kingsize bed so much that we drove an extra hundred miles today just so we could stay here again tonight. I hope it's not already taken."

"My goodness, you remember me from two years ago?" she said. "That's a real compliment. And you say you drove a hundred extra miles just to stay with us again tonight? Well, to tell the truth, room six was reserved, but I just can't let someone else have *your* room, now can I? Besides, the other party's about half-an-hour late already. I'll give them number eight. It has a queensize bed."

I'm not implying you should pay a stranger a compliment just to get something out of him. I've complimented a man on his car . . . a woman on her hairdo or her dress . . . a store clerk on her courtesy . . . and I wasn't trying to get preferential treatment out of any of them. Of course, I did get a smile and that in itself was well worth the extra small effort I went to.

But if you do want to see the service improve next time you're in a restaurant or a busy department store, pay the person an unexpected compliment on anything at all and see for yourself how good things will start to happen for you right then and there.

How to Get a Total Stranger to Do as You Ask

If you want to be able to control the actions and attitudes of total strangers with your miracle people power—if you want to get a person you've never met before to do whatever you ask him to do for you, then say something or do something that will help make the other person feel superior to you in some way.

The plain truth is that every person you meet feels that he is better than you in one way or another. A sure way to his heart is for you to let him know that you recognize his superiority.

I can well recall the time I went to a bait and tackle shop to buy my first salt water fishing rig. I simply didn't know where or how to begin. The clerk was busy with several other customers so he couldn't help me immediately.

I lifted one rod after another out of the rack only to put it back. Then I looked at lines and hooks and weights but I didn't know what to pick up or what to put down. I noticed a man on my left watching me sympathetically.

"Can you help me out?" I said. "I've never done any surf fishing before and I don't know where to start."

"Sure, let me give you a hand," he said. "I've got an hour before I go back to work. I'll be glad to show you the ropes."

"I hate to bother you," I said. "I don't want to burn up your lunch hour for you. But I sure could use some good advice."

"Don't worry about my lunch hour," he said. "The important thing is to get you fixed up with the right kind of fishing tackle."

So he proceeded to tell me all about the differences of the various kinds of fishing rods. Then he showed me the kind he used and recommended it for me. After that he selected the reel and showed me how to put it on the rod and how to use it. Then came the hooks, the weights, the line, the leader, a pair of fishing pliers, a scaler, a knife to fillet the fish, and so on.

He spent nearly an hour with me. We'd completed my shopping and he was showing me how to assemble it when he glanced at his watch. "I think you're all set," he said. "I have to get back to work."

"I surely appreciate your help," I said. "I don't know what I'd have done without you. But I'm afraid I used up your entire noon hour. I'm sorry."

"Forget it," he said. "I'm just glad I was able to help you out."

If you'll just be willing to admit that people can be superior to you in some way, and then ask for their help, you'll soon find out that a tremendous number of benefits will come your way.

Ralph Waldo Emerson once said, "Every man I meet is in some way my superior; in that I can learn of him." Remember that idea and you'll have no trouble at all in putting this technique to work so you can gain the benefits for yourself.

How to Make Friends with a Total Stranger

Are you afraid to meet new people? Do you worry that they might not like you? Do you think they might not find you interesting because you've never been anywhere or done anything important? You have no reason at all to be concerned. Let me show you how you can make friends instantly and impress a total stranger with your personality wherever you go.

I was recently invited to a small informal gathering at a friend's house. My hostess introduced me as a "real live author" to a good looking young lady named Jo Ann who was her house guest.

"A writer. How nice," said this young woman, and I could tell by the sound of her voice that a "real live author" was the last thing in this whole wide world she was interested in.

"You have a gorgeous tan," I said to her. "And right in the middle of winter, too. How did you do it? Where have you been—Miami Beach . . . Mexico . . . Hawaii?"

"Hawaii," she said. "Oh, it was so wonderful—so romantic."

"Tell me all about it," I said, and for the next two hours she did.

The next day my hostess called to say how much Jo Ann had enjoyed talking with me the night before. "She told me what an interesting person you were to talk with," she said. But I hadn't said more than ten words all night long. See what I mean?

So if you want to be known as an excellent conversationalist, if you want to make friends instantly with a total stranger, all you need do is lead the other person into talking about *himself,* and *his* interests, *his* business, *his* golf score, *his* successes, *her* children, *her* hobbies, *her* trip, and so on. Do that, listen with rapt attention, and people will love you for it.

They'll remember you, too, and sooner or later good things are bound to come your way. Take Jo Ann, for instance. She wanted one of my books—autographed, of course—to show her friends. Heaven only knows how many people will buy one of my books as a result of my listening patiently and attentively to her for a couple of hours. Do the same, and you, too, will be able to gain the benefits of being a good listener.

How to Control People's Attitudes and Emotions

When you study electricity, physics, or chemistry, you find that positive attracts negative, like goes with unlike, acid neutralizes alkali, and so on. But this doesn't hold true in the study of human relationships. When you're dealing with people, just the opposite is true. Let me show you exactly what I mean:

- Be kind to others . . . they will be kind to you.
- Be mean to others . . . they will be mean to you.
- Be courteous to others . . . they will be courteous to you.
- Be rude to others . . . they will be rude to you.
- Be friendly with others . . . they will be friendly with you.
- Be hostile to others . . . they will be hostile toward you.
- Smile at others . . . they will smile at you.
- Frown at others . . . they will frown at you.

With human beings it's strictly monkey see—monkey do. Like attracts like. Anger attracts anger. Love attracts love. The attitudes and emotions of other people depend entirely on your attitude and your emotions. The potential power you have over others and your ability to control their emotions is enormous. You can use it or misuse it. It's all up to you.

"If you lose your temper and yell at another person, he can't help but yell back at you," says Fred Morgan, a line supervisor with Southern Bell Telephone Company. "You invite retaliation and you'll darned well get it, too.

"The trouble is, the louder you yell, the angrier you get, and the angrier you get the louder you yell. The same thing happens to the other person so you end up with nothing but a shouting match where nobody wins.

"You can control another person's emotions with your own, and that's for sure. What you get back depends entirely upon what you give away."

In dealing with people, you'll always see your own attitude reflected back in the other person's behavior. It is almost as if you were looking at yourself in a mirror. When you smile, the man in the mirror smiles. When you frown, he frowns back at you.

Take my four year old grandson, Adam Lucas, just for example. When I smile at him, he's happy, and he smiles, too. But if I frown the least little bit or if I act irritated and impatient about something, he gets a worried look on his face, and he'll say, "Are you mad, grandpa?" I'll smile back at him and reply, "No, of course I'm not mad. Are you?" A look of relief and joy will come into his face and he'll say, "Nope—I'm not mad either. I'm happy!"

Smiles and frowns are both contagious. It's all up to you how you want to infect the other person. His attitude and his emotions depend entirely on your attitude and your emotions.

How to Control the Actions of Other People

If you want people to do a certain thing, if you want them to take some specific action, then you should do it first yourself. You must lead the way and set the example to be followed.

Before becoming a top life insurance salesman and a perennial best selling author, Frank Bettger was a baseball player until an accident on the playing field stopped short his athletic career. But Mr. Bettger learned much from his baseball playing days that he was able to apply to his later life. He tells about this in his book, *How I Raised Myself from Failure to Success in Selling.*[1]

Mr. Bettger had started with the Tri-State League playing for the Johnstown, Pennsylvania, team. He was young, ambitious, and anxious to get to the top. But instead he was fired. He went to the manager to ask why and was told it was because he was too lazy.

"You drag yourself around the field like a veteran who's been playing ball for twenty years," the manager told him. "Why do you act that way if you're not lazy?"

"Well, Bert," Mr. Bettger said, "I'm so nervous, so scared, that I want to hide my fear from the crowd and from the other players. I thought by taking it easy, I'd get rid of my nervousness."

"It'll never work, Frank," the manager said. "That's what's hold-

---

[1] Frank Bettger, *How I Raised Myself from Failure to Success in Selling*, Englewood Cliffs, New Jersey, Prentice-Hall, Inc., 1949.

ing you down. Whatever you do after you leave here, for heaven's sake, wake up, and put some life and enthusiasm into your work."

Later on, Mr. Bettger tried out with the New Haven, Connecticut, team. "My first day in New Haven will always stand out in my memory as a great event in my life," Mr. Bettger says. "No one knew me in that league, so I made a resolution that nobody would ever accuse me of being lazy."

"From the moment I appeared on the field, I acted like a man electrified. I acted as though I were alive with a million batteries. I threw the ball around the diamond so fast and so hard it almost knocked our infielders' hands apart. Once, apparently trapped, I slid into third base so fast and so hard the third baseman fumbled the ball and I was able to score an important run.

"Did it work? It worked like magic. Here's what happened:

"1. My enthusiasm almost entirely overcame my fear. In fact, my nervousness began to work for me, and I played far better than I ever thought I was capable of playing.
"2. My enthusiasm affected the other players on the team, and they too became enthusiastic.

"My biggest thrill came the following morning when I read the New Haven newspaper for it said, 'This new player, Bettger, has a barrel of enthusiasm. He inspired our boys. They not only won the game, but they looked better than at any time this season.' "

You can see from this how the actions of the other players—none of whom had ever met Frank Bettger before that day—were completely influenced, dominated, and controlled by Mr. Bettger's actions. They did as he did. They followed his example.

So if you want to use your miracle people power to dominate and control the actions of others, you must do the same. You must set the example. Force yourself to act enthusiastic and you'll become enthusiastic. What's more, the people around you will become enthusiastic, too.

11

How to Use Miracle People Power to Overcome Anger and Bitterness, Suspicion and Mistrust

If a person is angry or bitter, or if he views you with suspicion and mistrust, it will usually be for one of several reasons. It may be because of something you've said or done. It could also be because of something he *thinks* you've said or done.

Then at times, a person will take out his anger at the organization —for example, the company or corporation, the government, even society—on you because you happen to be the closest target. Finally, some people's imaginations work overtime. They think that everybody is against them or out to get them.

But no matter what the cause, I want to show you how to—

1. Turn off a person's anger and bitterness immediately.
2. Discover the reason behind his anger and bitterness—his suspicion and mistrust.
3. Turn anger and bitterness into love and friendship.
4. Get rid of a person's suspicion and mistrust.
5. Handle a person who's reached his breaking point.
6. Appease the person who's mad at the whole world.
7. Overcome your own anger and bitterness toward others.

These are some mighty big *benefits you'll gain* when you use your miracle people power to overcome anger and bitterness, suspicion and mistrust. Now let's go over each one of them in detail so I can show you—

HOW TO PUT THESE TECHNIQUES TO WORK
SO YOU CAN GAIN THE BENEFITS

How to Turn Off a Person's Anger and Bitterness Immediately

When a person becomes angry with you, you have your choice of doing one of two things. You can retaliate, get mad, and fight back, or you can do exactly the opposite—appease his anger.

If you fight back—which is exactly what the other person expects you to do—you will lose complete control of the situation and only make things worse. You will accomplish absolutely nothing by losing your temper. In fact, the inability to control your temper indicates a definite lack of self-discipline. And if you cannot control yourself, you cannot expect to control others.

What happens, then, if you don't fight back? Does this mean the other person automatically wins? Of course not. The only time you can be sure of winning is when you don't lose your temper and retaliate. It always takes at least two to make a fight. When you refuse to become angry, the other person's anger has to burn itself out.

Gary Nichols says—

"I have a neighbor with a short fuse who flies off the handle at any excuse. Used to be when he came over raising the dickens about something, I'd get mad, yell back, and we'd get nowhere. We fought like cats and dogs until I learned how to handle him. Now when he gets upset or mad at me, I fly off into a great calm instead of a great rage. When I refuse to fight, he realizes he might just as well cuss out a tree or a bush so he throws in the towel and gives up."

So you see, the best way to turn off a person's anger immediately is to respond in a kind and friendly manner. Remain calm and say nothing for a few moments until he's emotionally drained himself. Then answer him quietly and softly for as the Bible says, "A soft answer turneth away wrath," and that's true. If you use a soft tone of voice, it will not only calm down the other person, but it will keep you from getting angry, too.

When you refuse to fight back, when you speak softly, the angry person suddenly realizes he's the only one yelling. This embarrasses him and makes him feel awkward. He suddenly becomes extremely selfconscious and anxious to get the situation back to normal as quickly as possible.

You can use these facts of applied psychology to control and quiet down the other person's emotions to an amazing degree. So when you find yourself in a tense situation that threatens to get completely out of hand, deliberately lower your voice and keep it down. This in turn will motivate the other person to lower his own voice. As long as he speaks softly, he cannot remain angry and emotionally high-strung for very long.

Once you have him quieted down, you can then move on to the next technique which will show you—

How to Discover the Reason Behind His Anger and Bitterness, His Suspicion and Mistrust

As I said in the beginning of this step, when a person is angry with you, it will usually be for one of several reasons. It could be because of something you've said or done. It could also be because of something he *thinks* you've said or done. Sometimes he'll take his anger out on you even though he's upset with someone else. Occasionally, the person will have a persecution complex and thinks the whole world—including you—is out to get him. No matter what the cause of his anger is, it's up to you to find it so you can correct it.

"An angry or disgruntled employee cannot do his work properly," says Dallas Collins, the Director of Industrial Relations for Midland Steel in Gary, Indiana. "I always use the *Five W's of Intelligence* to determine what the angry person's problem is, and I insist that our foremen and supervisors do the same thing.

"I make every effort to get to the bottom of things immediately by asking questions of *what, who, when, where, why,* or *how*. I want to know *why* the person is angry . . . *what made him mad* . . . *who* is responsible for doing it . . . *when* and *where* it happened . . .

and *what* I can do to help him get rid of his anger and bitterness. I keep on plugging until I get the answers so I can resolve the person's problem.

"Time is always of the essence in taking care of an employee's gripes. If a person is angry and his anger is not appeased or his problem is not solved promptly, he'll end up carrying a grudge. So we do our best to take care of a bad situation as fast as possible to keep it from getting any worse."

I, too, have always used the *who, what, when, where,* and *why* system of questioning to discover the reason behind a person's anger and bitterness, or his suspicion and mistrust. I also use one additional question even when I think I've got all the answers and that is, "Is there any other reason for you to be upset about this?"

This will usually wring the last bit of anger and bitterness out of a person. I will expend all my efforts to discover why a person is upset with me, for I have no desire to be at odds with anybody. If you, too, want no enemies, I recommend that you do the same.

How to Turn Anger and Bitterness into Love and Friendship

To say you're sorry, even when you're at fault, seems to come hard to many people. But when you're wrong, you should promptly admit it. I know of no faster way to change anger and bitterness into love and friendship than to apologize to the person whose feelings you've hurt.

"One time I had occasion to write to a lawyer with whom I was most unhappy," says Grant McCullough. "I guess I got carried away and my letter became a little more caustic than I meant it to be.

"At any rate, he called to tell me in no uncertain terms what he thought of my remarks. He was really angry about my letter and he laid it on hot and heavy. When he paused for breath, I cut in and said, 'Vic, I'm truly sorry I wrote that letter. I should never have done it. I'm sorry and I apologize for what I said. I was absolutely wrong; you're completely right for being upset about it.'

"He was quiet for a few moments and then he said, 'That's all right, Grant. I admire you for having the guts to say you're wrong. I'm sorry, too. Let's be friends and start all over, okay?' "

As you can see, to promptly admit your mistake when you're wrong and apologize to the person you've hurt can immediately turn his anger and bitterness into love and friendship. But you can go even further than that for even better results. All you need do is *say you're sorry even when you're not wrong.*

"Love means never having to say you're sorry is a concept that's been quite popular in recent years," says Doctor Herman Palmer, a marriage counselor from Rockford, Illinois. "But I can't go along with that idea at all. *True love means saying you're sorry and taking the blame for things even when you're not wrong.*

"I have couples come to me for help all the time when all they need do to solve their problems is for each one to tell the other that they're sorry, *no matter who's at fault.* But neither one will give ground; neither one is willing to do that. Each one insists on being right and won't apologize to the other person.

"What difference does it make who's right or who's wrong if you really do love each other? Say you're sorry even when you're not at fault. Apologize even when you know that you're right. It's the quickest way I know to repair an argument with someone you love and save a marriage all at the same time."

Not only will Dr. Palmer's method save a lot of marriages, but it will also save a lot of friendships. When you're not in the wrong, you can afford to be big about things. If just saying you're sorry will restore peace in the family, or in the group, or between two friends, then say it and get on with the more important business of enjoying each other's companionship.

How to Get Rid of a Person's Suspicion and Mistrust

It is plain old human nature for people of one group to look at people of another group with suspicion and mistrust. If you happen to be a Democrat, you don't trust a Republican; if you're a Republican, you view a Democrat with suspicion. In North Ireland, Catholics hate Protestants and vice-versa.

Examples of groups who look at other groups with suspicion and mistrust are almost endless: officers and enlisted men in the armed services; management and labor in business and industry; black people and white people; medical doctors and chiropractors.

If a person views you with suspicion and mistrust just because you represent a certain group or a particular class of people, here's a method I picked up from Doctor Walter G. Bonner, a chiropractor in Springfield, Missouri, that you can use to change his attitude.

"I've been introduced to people time and again who tell me they don't believe in chiropractic or that they don't trust chiropractors," Dr. Bonner says. "I don't argue with them about it. That would be a complete waste of my time.

"Instead, I simply say, 'Tell me, Mrs. Jones, do you ever eat eggs?' When she says *yes,* then I say, 'Have you ever got hold of a bad one?' Of course, her answer is *yes* again. So then I say, 'Well, you don't have to worry about me . . . I'm one of the good ones.'

"That never fails to work. I may not gain Mrs. Jones as a patient right away, but I have gained her as a friend. Usually, she will start asking questions and I can explain the chiropractic theory to her easily for now she's receptive to me and my ideas. I could never overcome her suspicion and mistrust of the chiropractic profession by arguing with her about it."

This method can be used to combat a person's suspicion and mistrust no matter what or who you are—preacher, teacher, policeman, politician, used car salesman, or whatever. And it's a natural for a door-to-door salesman to use so he can overcome a housewife's normal inclination to view him with suspicion.

Now if you've done something yourself that warrants and deserves another person's suspicion and mistrust, that's something else again. Then the best way out is to tell the other person the absolute truth. Put all your cards on the table and back up your statements with proof and indisputable facts.

How to Handle the Person
Who's Reached His Breaking Point

Every person has his own emotional breaking point just as he has his own individual pain threshold. Some can take more than others, but sooner or later, all of us will reach the point of no return where we simply cannot stand any more pain or criticism or punishment of any sort. Let me give you an example of how to handle a person who has reached that breaking point.

"Back in the Korean War, I learned a lesson that has helped me tremendously during my years here with General Dynamics," says Russell B. Oliver, vice-president in charge of research and development. "At that time I was a battalion supply officer in the infantry. We were on maneuvers in the field and on the last day we were to haul the kitchens back to the camp after the breakfast meal so we could use the trucks to carry troops.

"The H Company mess sergeant just couldn't seem to get organized that morning. He'd been chewed out by his company commander, the executive officer, the mess officer, and the first sergeant for being late. Then my battalion supply sergeant came along and took a bite out of him for holding up the convoy. Before we pulled out I had a crack at him, too. We finally took off for the post without him. I left orders for him to hightail it back to camp as fast as he could.

"I waited back in the battalion garrison area for him. As soon as I saw the H Company truck come in, I headed for their messhall. But instead of unloading the truck right away, Sergeant King and his cooks and KPs had gone over to the barracks to get rid of their equipment—their packs and rifles.

"Well, I landed all over him and told him to get his truck unloaded before he did anything else. But Sergeant King had had it. He looked me straight in the eye and said, 'Damn it, Lieutenant, I've had all I can take this morning from officers. You can go straight to hell!'

"I realized it was no use for me to talk to him any further at that moment so I left, saying that I'd see him back in the field. The next day he came to my office to apologize for his conduct. I accepted his apology and told him to forget the incident. Some officers would have had him court-martialed, I know, but as far as I was concerned, he was far too good a man for that.

"I knew he'd simply reached his emotional breaking point that morning and that he would get over it. And of course he did. I served with Sergeant King for more than two years in the 19th Infantry. He was one of the finest soldiers I ever met.

"Whenever I'm tempted to be too harsh on some of our people who also have reached their own breaking point, I think back to Sergeant King, and I've been able to restrain myself from taking some drastic action that I would regret later on. I don't want to lose any good people just because they had a few bad moments."

If you have a person who reaches his emotional threshold, you should do the same. Don't fight back. Let him get it all out of his system. The important thing is to clear up the disagreement in such a way that good feelings and a warm friendly relationship can be restored after the storm has passed.

How to Appease the Person
Who's Mad at the Whole World

Once in a while you'll run into the person who feels he's been had by society, government, big business, or by someone. He's mad at the whole world. No one can do anything right. You'll need a lot of patience to handle a person who's deeply embittered like that. You will also need a tremendous amount of tact and diplomacy to draw the real reason for his hostility out of him.

Carl Porter, a general foreman with the Delco-Remy Division of General Motors Corporation in Anderson, Indiana, had a man like that. I'd like Carl to tell you about him.

"We had a worker by the name of Dean in our department who was really teed-off at the whole world," Carl says. "He was a constant complainer . . . nothing was ever quite right for him. The punch press he operated didn't suit him. The material he was given to run was always bad, he said.

"Dean despised and resented authority fiercely. It made him hopping mad if a supervisor watched him or checked his work. He had a don't-give-a-damn-attitude and his work record reflected that. He was an extremely hard man to get to know.

"Well, I was determined to get inside his mind to find out what was eating at him. Week after week of strictly one-sided conversations went by. Little by little I pieced together his background. He was violently bitter toward society. Every so often he would go out and really tie one on—evidently trying to wipe out the past and its unpleasant memories, which seemed to be many.

"Finally, I learned that he'd been in prison for nearly two years. Then I really hit the jackpot. Dean had been innocent and had been falsely imprisoned. Although he had received a full pardon from the governor and monetary restitution from the state, he was still extremely angry and bitter that society had wronged him this way. As a result, he hated everybody viciously and trusted no one.

"But after Dean found someone to talk to about this horrible experience in his life, he began to change rapidly for the better. Evidently I was the outlet he needed to get rid of all his stored-up hatred and venom. He seemed to burn all the old resentments out of his system simply by opening up and talking to me. Once he was free of the past, he was able to start a brand-new life for himself."

No two people will respond alike when they're mad at the whole world, but I will guarantee this. Practice the healing art of paying sympathetic attention to the other person, listen patiently with tolerance and understanding, and you'll be able to help him so he can solve his problem of anger and bitterness, suspicion and mistrust by himself.

How to Overcome Your Own Anger and Bitterness Toward Others

The Bible says never to let the sun go down on your wrath, and that's mighty good advice. Prolonged anger and bitterness come from hanging onto your resentments. And the real problem is that being constantly angry with another person doesn't hurt him one bit —it only hurts you.

You're the one who develops peptic ulcers and high blood pressure from your anger—not the person with whom you're upset. Let me tell you a little story here that will help you learn how *not* to hang onto your resentments or carry a grudge.

"I'm a recovered alcoholic," Dick S. says, "and I have to be careful of *stinkin' thinkin'*. I was really up tight one night and filled with resentment when I went to my regular Alcoholics Anonymous meeting.

"One of my friends, Norman P., noticed how tense I was and asked me what was wrong. Well, I told him what a tough day I'd had . . . how the boss had called me in his office the first thing that morning and how he'd chewed me out unmercifully . . . how he made me feel like a fool . . . how it made me miserable all day long . . . how I was still feeling rotten about it all.

" 'Gee, it must have been pretty bad to upset you that much,' Norman said. 'How long did your boss have you on the carpet?'

" 'About ten minutes,' I said.

" 'Ten minutes!' Norman said in astonishment. 'Ten minutes is all? Hell, Dick, you didn't have a bad day. You just had a bad ten minutes, but you nursed it all day!' "

12

How You Can Use Your Miracle People Power to Gain the Complete Confidence of Everyone

You just passed the half-way mark in Miracle People Power when you read Chapter 11—*How to Use Miracle People Power to Overcome Anger and Bitterness, Suspicion and Mistrust.*

So before you read *How You Can Use Your Miracle People Power to Gain the Complete Confidence of Everyone*, I think it would be wise for you to take a bit of a breather so you can see where you've been and where you're going.

With that thought in mind, then, let's review the first eleven chapters for just a minute. Some of them were used to show you how to improve your powers of observation and to increase your ability to analyze and understand the words and actions of other people.

For instance, Chapter 1 pointed out to you how important it is to determine exactly what a person's innermost needs and desires are so you can use that information for your own benefit.

In Chapter 2, I told you how you could use your knowledge of these innermost needs and desires to influence and control every one you meet.

Chapter 3 gave you the reverse side of the coin of desire—fear—and showed you how you could use it to increase your miracle people power so you could get what you want.

I included Chapter 4 early in the sequence to help you determine when, where, and on whom to concentrate your attention so you wouldn't waste your time on the wrong person, while Chapter 5 came next so you could use your miracle people power tool of listening in on your selected targets to get results. Chapter 6 served as the cap for those initial steps for it showed you how to use what you'd already learned so you could get your own way every time.

Chapters 7, 8, and 9 should always be considered as a group for they cover how to use words that will double and triple your miracle people power in everything you write and say.

Along that same line, Chapter 10 shows you how to control the actions and attitudes of complete strangers by what you say and do, while the chapter you just finished gave you valuable information on how to say the right thing at the right time to overcome anger and bitterness, suspicion and mistrust.

That small review brings us right up-to-date. Now for the future. Chapters 12 through 19 will be used primarily to give you concrete and exact miracle people power techniques that you can use to solve specific problems of human relationships—like gaining the confidence of others . . . getting cooperation and support from your co-workers . . . how to win an argument every time . . . how to use a technique that will work when all other methods fail . . . how to issue orders that get miraculous results . . . how to criticize people tactfully to prevent hard feelings . . . and finally—how to get the best out of people.

Then the last two chapters deal strictly with you and your own personal life. Chapter 20 shows you how you can use your miracle people power to improve your own family life, while Chapter 21 tells you how to sustain your own miracle people power at a high level all the time.

Now that you have your second wind, let's get with it again.

BENEFITS YOU'LL GAIN
WHEN PEOPLE HAVE CONFIDENCE IN YOU

When People Trust You, They'll Accept Your Leadership

When you show by your words and your actions that you have absolute confidence in yourself and in the successful completion of any task, no matter how difficult it might seem to be, people will trust you. They'll accept your leadership and follow your example. They will adopt the same measure of confidence that you show. Your faith in their abilities will encourage them to apply their full powers to the job that's to be done.

You'll Get Things Done

When you tackle a difficult problem with confidence and enthusiasm, you will encourage others to adopt a similar attitude. You will be able to get things done, for people work best for those in whom they have confidence and trust. When you display such confidence yourself, you can say, "This is what we have to do. Here's how we're going to do it. Now let's go to it."

You'll Save Time, Energy, and Effort

When you show confidence in people to get the job done, you'll get far better work out of them. So if you're going to give someone a vote of confidence, then go all out. You'll be amazed at the extent of their capabilities. This principle will work to solve all sorts of difficult problems. The more confidence you show in people, the more confidence they'll have in themselves to do the job, and the less time, energy, and effort you'll have to expend in supervising them and their work to get the job done.

Your Miracle People Power Will Expand and Increase

If you want people to trust you and have confidence in you, you must trust them and have confidence in them first. Just as I said back in Chapter 10, like attracts like, remember? You can show by your words and actions that you trust people and that you have confidence in their abilities to get the job done. That kind of attitude will be reflected back toward you from them, and your own miracle people power will be expanded and increased as a result.

TECHNIQUES YOU CAN USE TO GAIN THESE BENEFITS

How to Be the Technical Expert in Your Own Field

The person who knows his business inside out, who is the technical expert and the authority in his own field, has complete confidence in himself and in his own abilities. Usually, such confidence comes from extensive study, research, and long experience.

For instance, if you want to increase your self-confidence, you will constantly continue to improve yourself. Don't stop studying just because you've graduated from school and have your degree. You'll never live long enough to know everything there is to know about your chosen profession. As Henry Ford once said, "Anyone who stops learning is old—whether at twenty or eighty. Anyone who keeps learning stays young. The greatest thing in life is to keep your mind young."

So continue to study, to read, and to research into every corner of your chosen field. If you're not working, but you still want to improve yourself by other than your own reading at home, then take some correspondence courses or attend some night schools.

I have two neighbors, both in their mid-forties, who are currently taking some adult education courses at Drury College. Sam is taking a course in creative expression so he can improve his writing and speaking skills. Frank is taking a course in applied psychology so he can improve his relationships with his co-workers.

To be an expert in your own field requires that you not only retain what you learned in school yesterday, but that you also keep up-to-date today and prepare yourself for tomorrow. No matter whether you're a foreman or a supervisor, a doctor or a lawyer, a teacher or a scientist, you'll have to keep on learning for there are constant technological changes every day.

Nothing is ever static. Time stands still for no one. The only thing constant is change. Progress is continuous. If you want to hold your position as an authority in your own field, so you can retain the confidence of people, you'll need to keep up and continue your professional education and development. There simply is no other way.

My own family doctor, Dr. Griffin, last year closed his practice for two months so he could attend some postgraduate courses at the University of Iowa. And Doc is in his mid-fifties and has been in practice now for more than twenty-five years.

How to Increase Your Confidence in Dealing with Others

When you're an expert and the authority in your own field, when you know your business better than anyone else, there is no reason at all for you to lack confidence in dealing with other people.

However, I do know that some persons are extremely bashful or afraid to speak up in front of a group of people and express an opinion, even when they're absolutely certain of their facts and sure of their statistics.

If you have this problem, if you're bashful or afraid of others, if you lack confidence in dealing with people, then I can tell you that the solution to your problem is simply to do what you're afraid of doing until you're no longer afraid to do it.

If you will remember, I told you back in Chapter 3 how to conquer fear. The first step was to admit your fear. The second one was to analyze your fear to see if it was justified. The last step was to take the necessary action to conquer your fear which usually will consist of doing the thing that you fear to do.

Some of the reasons most people give for lacking self-confidence in dealing with others are these: fear of expressing an opinion in front of a group; fear of making a mistake in front of others; fear of making the wrong decision; fear of what other people might think of them; fear of what others might say or do; fear of meeting strangers; fear of being conspicuous in front of others.

If any of these are weaknesses of yours, then you should take action to correct them. I would suggest strongly that you go back and read Chapter 3 over and over again until you have completely rid yourself of your fear.

But for now, let me give you a quick for instance to show you how you can tackle one of your weaknesses. As I said, a lot of people have an inner fear of being conspicuous. For example, have you ever noticed how the back seats of a church, a classroom, or an assembly hall always fill up first? Do you know why? Well, most people try to sit in the back where they won't be seen, noticed, or called upon because they lack confidence in themselves and in their own abilities.

If you've been in the habit of doing this, then it's one of your weaknesses that you need to work on. So sit up front next time. It will build your self-confidence to do what you're afraid of doing. And make it a point from now on to sit as close to the front as you can. A simple little action like this can be the beginning of a new self-confidence and more miracle people power for you.

How to Radiate Your Confidence to Others

If you have confidence in yourself and faith in your own abilities, that fact will literally radiate from you. It will be evident in everything you say and do. As a result, people are bound to have confidence in you.

What makes a successful doctor, lawyer, or salesman? Confidence in himself and enthusiasm for what he's doing more than anything else in the whole world. Oh sure, he has to know his stuff, I grant you that, but I've seen some of the brainiest people in the world fail because they lacked faith in themselves and in their own abilities.

I can well remember when I had a low back problem some years ago. Braces, plasters, and several weeks in traction in a hospital had done no good at all. So I went to see a chiropractor.

This doctor was a brilliant man, no doubt about that. He had graduated from his chiropractic college magna cum laude. A framed certificate hanging on the wall in his private office said so. He had also taken a variety of chiropractic postgraduate courses as evidenced by a number of diplomas and certificates of attendance that I saw.

But when I told him about my condition and asked him if he could help me, he was hesitant and doubtful. "Well, I don't know," he said. "That all depends on whether your case is a chiropractic one or not. I might be able to help you if it is. Then again, I might not. I'll try, however. I'll do my best and we'll see what happens. Maybe a couple of treatments might do the trick, and then again—maybe not. I just don't know . . . I'm not really sure . . . we'll just have to wait and see . . ."

Well, I left his office without getting an adjustment. This chiropractor had no confidence in himself and his own abilities, so as a result, neither did I.

But my back still hurt and I had to do something. My wife said, "He's not the only chiropractor in town. Why don't you go to see Doctor Laneville down on Main Street? He must be good. His office is always full."

So I went to see the second chiropractor. After four hours of waiting, I finally got in to see him. What a difference in doctors. It was immediately apparent. This one radiated confidence. He was bubbling over with enthusiasm for his work. He told me of the people he had helped . . . of the ailments he had cured. When I told him what was wrong and asked if he could help me, he looked at me in open-mouthed astonishment and said, "Help you? Of course I can help you! What in the dickens do you think I'm in practice here for?"

PS: I stayed. He cured my backache.

How to Win and Hold the Confidence of Others

There is no better way to win and hold a person's confidence than to tell him the whole truth. By the same token, there is no quicker way to lose his confidence and trust than to lie to him. So if you're going to use your miracle people power to inspire people to have confidence in you and to trust you, then follow these five simple guidelines:

1. Practice Absolute Honesty and Truthfulness at All Times.
I can think of no exception to this rule whatever. Of course, this
doesn't mean that you should intentionally insult a person or hurt his
feelings by telling the truth. If you can say nothing good about a
person, then do exactly that: say nothing. Just take your own inventory—not someone else's. If you're like me, that will keep you quite
busy enough.

2. Make Your Word Your Bond. If you want people to have full
and absolute confidence in you, then your word must be your bond.
To make sure you always keep your word, keep these three simple
points in mind:

1. Never make a promise you cannot keep.
2. Never make a decision you cannot support.
3. Never issue an order you can't enforce.

3. Be Accurate and Truthful in All Your Written Statements.
You should also keep in mind that your signature on any document
or any piece of correspondence is just as important as what you say
to a person face-to-face. When you sign a check, your signature is
your certificate that you have money in the bank. Your signature in
your work and in your business must carry the same weight.

4. Stand for What You Believe to Be Right. Have the courage
of your convictions, no matter what the consequences. Never compromise your standards; never prostitute your principles. If you
ever are tempted to compromise, then place honesty, your sense of
duty, and personal honor above all else.

5. Be Ready to Accept the Blame if You Are Wrong. If you're
wrong, have the courage to say so. Always be ready and willing to
take the blame at all times if you did make the mistake. Accept the
blame when you know full well that you are the one who is really
at fault.

Here's a Sure-Fire Way to Gain People's Confidence

The most important thing a trial lawyer can do in pleading his
case in court is to *bring on his witnesses.* Naturally the judge and
jury feel the lawyer is prejudiced in his views. If he is the prosecuting
attorney, he sees things far differently than if he were on the side of

the defendant. So most things a lawyer says are not taken at strictly
face value. He has to prove his case to win the confidence of his
listeners. This he does by calling his witnesses to the stand to verify
that what he says is true.

You can also use witnesses outside the courtroom to establish the
confidence of others in what you say and do. For instance, one
winter we decided to spend January and February in Arizona. We
had a travel trailer to live in. I wrote to a dozen different trailer
parks in Phoenix and the surrounding area requesting information
on their services and facilities.

Eleven of them sent back beautifully printed colored brochures
and form letters telling me what they had to offer. The twelfth one
sent me a brochure, too, but he also enclosed a personal letter with
the names and addresses of people in Missouri who'd spent winters
with him before. Four of those names were people who lived right in
my own town of Springfield.

"Please call any of these people," the letter said. "They can tell
you, far better than any brochure, what I can offer you and whether
you'd enjoy staying with us or not." You know where we spent the
winter, of course.

I know a successful mail order dealer in New Jersey, Jack Stone,
who has built a big business selling boots and shoes. He started from
scratch and is now grossing more than one million dollars every
year. He uses one procedure that he emphasizes above all others:
witnesses.

Jack will not let a letter go out that does not have the name and
address of at least one satisfied customer in the town—or at least
nearby—to which he's mailing his advertisement. At first, of course,
it was difficult for him to do that. He did not have thousands of
satisfied customers to refer to as he has today.

So in the beginning he had to gain a person's confidence by offering a good product on a "free-trial-no-money-down-try-it-for-10-
days" plan. That helped to establish his business and get him started.

But just as soon as 30 days passed without the customer returning
the merchandise, Jack would write a personal letter to him asking
for a testimonial in return. He used these letters to establish confidence in himself and his products by including the names and
addresses in new letters that he mailed out. And it worked. Jack
credits his mail-order success to this more than anything else. "It's

the quickest way to gain a potential customer's confidence," he says. "Witnesses convert prospects into solid customers."

Back in Chapter 9, I told you how to write letters that were loaded with miracle people power. If you're writing a sales letter, this information should be used along with the techniques I gave you back there.

How to Increase Your Self-Confidence and People's Confidence in You All at the Same Time

Why does a woman buy a new hat or a new dress when she's feeling low and down in the dumps? Because it makes her look better, feel better, and restores her confidence in herself and in her appearance.

If you're feeling depressed, if you're making calls and not selling anything, if you lack faith in yourself and in your own abilities, if people have no confidence in you, maybe all you need do to snap yourself out of it is buy a new tie, a new shirt, or a new pair of shoes.

You see, it's important that you look the part. Sometimes that's more than half the battle of winning the confidence of others. How you dress, act, and carry yourself can actually radiate your authority and self-confidence to others.

Clay Tillman, a senior pilot for a leading airline told me—

"We could fly our airplanes just as well wearing slacks and sport shirts. And our stewardesses wouldn't have to wear uniforms to serve meals to our passengers either.

"But do you know what would happen to the company if we dressed that way? Why, they'd be broke in a year. People would lose confidence in us and in our abilities to do the job. They wouldn't trust us. A uniform for an airplane pilot or a stewardess is part of our image. It helps to establish us as authorities and experts in our own field. People trust us and have confidence in us when we look the part."

You should look the part, too. It is a simple and easy, yet extremely valuable, method you can use to increase your miracle people power by inspiring the complete confidence of everyone in you.

13

How Miracle People Power Can Make Your Co-Workers Cooperate and Support You 110 Percent

Cooperation with others is one of the major factors of success, no matter what profession or occupation you're in. One of the first things a person learns when he goes to work is that all business is a cooperative enterprise. You must cooperate with someone and offer to do something for him if you want him in turn to cooperate with you and do something for you.

And this basic fact of human relationships doesn't apply only to business or earning a living. It applies to your entire life . . . to everything you do. In your personal life . . . in your family relationships . . . in your church, civic group, school, community, or whatever—you must cooperate with someone, and they must cooperate with you and support you if you are to accomplish successfully what you set out to do.

What it boils down to is that you simply cannot succeed in life without the help and cooperation of other people. If you want to get ahead in this old world, no matter what you do, you must get other people on your side first. And that's what this step to miracle people power is all about.

BENEFITS YOU'LL GAIN
WHEN YOU COOPERATE WITH PEOPLE

1. People will respect you and have confidence in you.
2. They'll give you their willing obedience, their loyal cooperation, and their whole-hearted support.
3. They'll work with initiative, ingenuity, and enthusiasm.
4. They'll work together as a team with high spirit and good morale—with conviction, purpose, and direction toward a common goal.
5. You'll make them feel they belong where they are.
6. They'll work as hard as you do to get the job done.

TECHNIQUES YOU CAN USE TO GAIN THESE BENEFITS

How Cooperation with People Will Pay Off for You

One of the problems in business and industry is that corporation and company managers, executives, and administrators at the top set up rules and regulations for workers at the bottom. But most people don't like being told what to do or what not to do. After all, rules are restrictions on their personal liberties. So they tend to resist those rules or disobey them.

One of the best ways you can cooperate with the people who work for you is to let them set up their own rules and regulations. You can have them coordinate with you or get your approval if you feel that's necessary. However, you'll usually find that the average person is much stricter on himself than you are. And since these rules are *his* rules, the ones *he* made up *himself,* he'll be much more likely to cooperate and follow them than if you made those same rules and regulations for him yourself.

General Foods, Motorola, Monsanto Chemical, just to mention a few, found this procedure to be highly profitable for them. For instance, the employees of the Gaines dogfood plant—a branch of General Foods in Topeka, Kansas—make most of their own rules. They have no time clocks or set hours for lunches or breaks. The work force is organized into teams who hire and fire their own members. Their whole operation is based on skill—not rules . . . results—not methods.

And those results, when compared with the statistics of other company plants run by conventional management methods, are extremely gratifying. Production is 40 percent higher in the Topeka plant than elsewhere. Absenteeism is down to less than 1 percent; in other plants, it runs as high as 10 percent. Sabotage is also a problem in other places. For instance, in the Kankakee, Illinois factory, someone dumped a batch of green dye into a hopper and spoiled an entire day's production of dogfood. In Topeka, workers discipline themselves and sabotage is unheard of.

In Monsanto Chemical's plant in Pensacola, Florida, the workers were allowed to reorganize the entire production system themselves. They literally became their own managers. Did this action on the part of the company motivate the employees to cooperate? You can judge for yourself. In the first year alone, waste dropped to zero and production jumped 50 percent.

The Motorola plant in Fort Lauderdale, Florida previously used a conventional assembly line system for their radio production. Absenteeism was high. So was employee turnover. Customer complaints about quality were far too numerous.

Then, cooperating fully with their own employees, Motorola allowed their workers to change and reorganize the system. Each employee became solely responsible for the entire manufacturing process of his own individual radios. He took care of the complete assembly of a receiver down to the final quality control checks and the actual packaging for shipment.

What were the results of this new system of mutual cooperation? Absenteeism and employee turnover dropped drastically. So did customer complaints. And Motorola found it had a team of happy, contented, and satisfied workers rather than a bunch of malicious malcontents.

Bell Telephone, Kaiser Steel, General Motors, Chrysler, Hewlett-Packard, and dozens of others are moving rapidly to give more responsibility and authority to their employees. Their methods are paying off for they are receiving better cooperation and support from their people.

If you want to obtain full cooperation and support from the

people who work with you or for you, then make them feel important and necessary, too. Ask questions, favors, opinions. Build up their status, their egos, their positions. Show them how and where they are vitally needed. Tell them how you can't get along without them. When you cooperate and work with your employees, your co-workers, your associates, and your friends this way, you'll receive the same benefits those big companies gained, too.

Use This Basic Method to Gain 110 Percent Cooperation from People

As you've already seen by the examples in the previous technique, there is no deep, dark, or hidden mystery about how to win the cooperation of other people. It simply boils down to this: *If you want to gain the cooperation and support of others, then you must give them your cooperation and support first.*

Successful people know that you must always give before you can get, and when you do, you always get back more than you give away. That's miracle people power in action.

So if you want cooperation and teamwork from people, then you must give them your cooperation and teamwork first. You can easily tell if you're doing that. If the people who work for you are prompt and cheerful, filled with enthusiasm, enjoy their jobs, and are ready to put in an extra hour or so when it's required, or when you ask them to do so—you can be sure you're doing the right thing.

But if you're not giving people your cooperation first, you can always tell that quite easily, too. They'll be just as disinterested in cooperating and getting along with you as you are with them. They'll drag into work late, be indifferent about their jobs, and run for the time clock before the whistle blows. If that's the way your people act, don't ask them for anything extra. You'll not get it.

Remember, then, *you must always give if you expect to get, and you always get back exactly what you give away, although the return is usually multiplied many times over.*

This idea is so important that it should be used in conjunction with every one of those twenty-one chapters to miracle people power. It should be kept in mind in all your daily contacts with other people—your employees, associates, co-workers, customers, friends, even your own family—for cooperation with others is a real key to miracle people power.

How to Get a Person to Go All Out for You

I want to show you two different methods people use to gain cooperation from others. Then you decide which one you want to use.

Method Number One. Say to a person, "Here's a job I want you to do for me." Then tell him exactly what you want done. Make sure he understands the job must be done your way and that no other way is satisfactory. You are not open to suggestion of any sort.

Method Number Two. Now say to a person, "Please help me figure out how to do this." In other words, don't tell him what's to be done. Ask him to tell you or to show you how to do it. This way you're asking for his brains as well as his physical efforts.

Now compare the results you get. With the first method, you will get only minimum cooperation and help—if you get any at all—for you're not asking the person for his opinion or advice. Instead, you're telling him what to do, and most people don't respond too well to orders and directives unless you use the techniques you'll learn in Chapter 16—*Miracle People Power Orders That Always Bring Miraculous Results.*

With the second method, you'll get 110 percent cooperation from the person for you're asking him for his ideas as well as his physical labor. And when people offer you their opinion or advice, it's hard for them to get their point across to you without actually showing you or physically helping you solve your problem.

How It Works

You can use this method on other than employees or subordinates to get the results you want. It works just as well on your friends and associates, too. I have a neighbor two doors down the street from me, a retired electrical contractor, who's a regular handy man around the house. Me—I'm all thumbs when it comes to sharpening knives or lawn mower blades, fixing a dripping faucet, repairing a faulty window latch, that sort of thing.

All I have to do is just ask Hal for his opinion or advice on any subject, and out comes the tool chest. He even made a half-dozen fishing leaders for me complete with hooks, sinkers, and all the trimmings when I barely mentioned how I wished I could catch fish the way he did.

You might ask what I'm giving Hal first to get all this cooperation and help from him. Fair enough, that's a good question and I'll answer it for you.

I'm fulfilling Hal's need for recognition of efforts; I'm offering him reassurance of worth. I'm letting him know he's still wanted and needed and appreciated by someone—something people especially crave after retirement. I'm also feeding his ego and giving him a sense of importance by asking him for his advice and his opinion. I give him a sense of personal power when he can do certain things far better than I can do them. And finally, I'm giving him dignity and a sense of self-esteem by showing respect for his abilities.

Look back in Chapter 1, and you'll find all those basic needs and desires every person has. Hal has them, I have them, and so do you. They form the base on which you can build your miracle people power.

All in all, I think it's a fair trade. I'm giving Hal something he needs and wants. I'm getting help, advice, and cooperation from him in return.

A Quick and Dependable Way to Get People to Cooperate and Work with You

If you want people to cooperate and work with you, then you must be a part of the team, too. You must be willing to share the same hardships, the same discomforts, and the same dangers they do. This is especially true if you work in a modern industrial plant.

If you think today's industrial plants are not dangerous to work in, you've never been inside a modern steel plant, a textile mill, or a rubber factory. Modern machinery, although highly efficient, can be deadly dangerous. I've seen enough workers with fingers, hands, and arms missing to know.

I'm not asking you to run a mixing mill, a drill press, or a rubber calendar if that's not your job. But I am saying that if you have an air-conditioned office while your employees must work in sweltering heat cooled only by ventilating fans, then you can cooperate and show your feeling for them by at least getting out there and sweating with them side by side once in a while.

They won't expect you to spend eight hours a day with them that way; that's not your job and they know it. But a simple act of cooperation like this will establish a bond of friendship and respect between you and your co-workers that you'll never gain in any other way.

"I never go through the plant but that I stop and lend a hand somewhere," says Ben Watson, assistant plant manager of the Springdale Rubber Company in Springfield, Missouri. "For instance, there's always a skid that has layers of rubber stuck to it. It's tough to get a layer of rubber off and into a mixing mill so whenever I see a millman sweating and tugging away at a stubborn skid, I stop and help him with it.

"Maybe it doesn't really help him very much, but we rub elbows and I get my hands dirty and we both part with a big fat grin for each other. And that's what I stopped for anyway."

Ben's method of lending a helping hand is especially good to use when you're setting out on a new project and people are a little backward about getting started. If you pitch in first, they'll cooperate with you and follow your lead.

Only one small note of caution is in order here, and that is: *When the boss gets too involved in the work, he's no longer the boss.* So you might keep that in mind. Before you get in too deep, be sure that you have a graceful way out.

A Sure Way to Get People to Support You

One of the best ways I know to get support and cooperation from people is to turn them loose when the job is done. Tell a person he can have the rest of the day off just as soon as he meets his quota with *quality* production and still get a full day's pay, and he'll work straight through his lunch hour so he can go home early.

A firm believer in this particular technique to gain cooperation and support from his employees is Arthur J. Decio, president of Skyline Corporation, one of the country's leading builders of top-quality mobile homes. Headquartered in Elkhart, Indiana, Skyline has 39 manufacturing and assembly plants throughout the United States.

Mr. Decio insists on fast quality production from his well-paid non-union work force. Morale is high. Each plant has a long waiting list of men and women who want to work for Skyline even though it is non-union. Here's why:

Skyline builds its homes only to order. Employees work until each day's quota—usually 18 to 20 mobile homes for each of the assembly plants across the country—is filled. Only then do they quit for the day. But this doesn't necessarily mean a long day. In fact, it can mean a short one, for if they're fast, they can leave early.

Nor does this mean that they can produce slipshod work and get by either. Skyline's quality control inspectors are the toughest in the business. Not only that, employees police their own ranks for people who are slow or lazy. They also eliminate the person who tries to shortcut or skip necessary production steps trying to speed up the production process. They know that if quality falls off, they will lose the privilege of quitting early, yet still getting paid for a full day's work.

How effective are Mr. Decio's methods of working with his employees to gain their cooperation and support? When he first took over the presidency of Skyline, annual sales were around 10 million. Today, they run 260 million, 26 times more than they were at first.

Skyline has gathered several industry firsts by using Decio's methods. It is number one in dollar sales of more than 400 builders in the mobile home industry. It also holds first place in the number of units manufactured. Among the 500 largest corporations in the United States, it holds down the number one position for return on shareholders' equity. Finally, it is completely debt-free, which without a doubt earns it a number one rating in this day and age.

If you want to get the same kind of cooperation and support from your people that Mr. Decio gets from his, then use this technique. As you can see from his track record, it's a proven winner.

How to Get This Kind of Cooperation in Your Home

What we've been talking about nearly all the way through this step is *participative management*. And it will work in your home for you and your family just as well as it works for Skyline, Motorola, Monsanto Chemical, General Foods, Springdale, and so on.

If you use participative management in your business and find it to be successful in gaining cooperation and support from your co-workers, then rest assured it'll work with your wife and children, too, if you'll just give it a chance to do so.

Dr. Roland J. Warner, a San Francisco psychiatrist says—

"A lot of husbands never tell their wives anything at all about their business, their work, or their plans for the future. They never give them a chance to make any kind of suggestion. Yet you'll hear them complain saying their wives won't cooperate with them in saving money, economizing, and so on. A lot of fathers think their children won't cooperate either, but the trouble is they never ask them to participate or to contribute any of their ideas. They only tell them what to do.

"I recommend to my patients with family problems that the husband, wife, and children get together at least once a month as a minimum for a family conference. At this meeting problems can be discussed, common goals established, and each person in the family can be asked to offer suggestions or to contribute his ideas.

"It is amazing to me how patients with seemingly insoluble family problems suddenly get better when they adopt this family participative management plan. Impossible situations get ironed out. The family gets along better. Everyone is much happier when each person is not told what to do or when to do it, but instead is asked for a solution to common family problems."

I recommend this method heartily. Although my own children are all grown and gone now, the family conference to get everybody's opinion and then vote on the problem has been our standard procedure for many years. I've always found that children will accept parental authority willingly, even when the decision goes against them just as long as they've had a chance to voice their opinions and make their suggestions known before the final vote is taken.

So take it from me. The family participative management plan is a good thing. Use it; you'll increase your miracle people power at home when you do.

14

Miracle People Power Techniques That Will Give You the Best of Every Argument

Almost every day, some circumstances will come up where you will need to get another person to accept your viewpoint or see things your way. Whether you accomplish that or not depends on which of the following two methods you use.

The first method—and the one most people use to try to win an argument—is *force*. If you use force in an attempt to overpower or intimidate your opponent, your argument will turn into nothing more than a shouting match and an ego battle.

Of course, when someone opposes your idea, especially when he does so vigorously, or when he uses threats and scare tactics or criticism and ridicule in an attempt to defeat you in an argument, it is only natural for you to become emotional and to respond in the same way.

But to do this is a complete waste of time. You cannot win an argument by forcefully ramming your ideas down the other person's throat or by trying to intimidate him. The only possible way you can ever really win an argument is when you get the other person to change his mind, which brings us to the second method—*persuasion*.

To win an argument every time, you must work with human nature—not against it. If you want a person to see things your way, don't try to force your ideas on him. He must accept your ideas from within himself—from inside his own mind. Your ideas must become *his* ideas before he will accept them. Once he's convinced himself that the viewpoint you present is correct, he'll change his mind voluntarily. Then when he sees things your way, when he makes your viewpoint *his* viewpoint, you'll win your argument.

You can get a person to accept your ideas within himself only when you appeal to his emotions as well as to his reason, his logic, and his common sense. As I told you back in Chapter 6, *the head never hears 'til the heart has listened.* You cannot possibly win an argument until that happens, and you will never win a person's heart by force—but only by persuasion.

Learning how to win an argument by using persuasion—not force —is the purpose of this step to miracle people power. When you know how to do that,

YOU'LL GAIN THESE BENEFITS

1. If you're a parent, you'll be able to persuade your children to adopt desirable behavior attitudes and patterns.
2. You can use the techniques in this step to get your husband to do what you want him to do when you're a wife, and that's a mighty big benefit for you.
3. When you're a manager, an employer, or a department head, you'll find that your subordinates will do things your way.
4. If you're a lawyer, you'll win your case by persuading the jury that you're right.
5. If you're a salesman, the proper use of this step will enable you to turn shaky prospects into solid customers.
6. Your students will be convinced of the value of your course if you're a teacher.
7. Even if you're a doctor, the techniques in this step will be valuable to you, for you can use them to get a patient to go along with your prescribed treatment.
8. No matter who you are or what you do, you'll be able to

benefit when you win an argument and get your own way
every time by using persuasion as one of your miracle people
power tools.

TECHNIQUES YOU CAN USE TO GAIN THESE BENEFITS

How to Retain Control of the Argument at All Times

Don't jump the gun and try to win an argument by stating your
side of the case first. If you do, you will reveal your position and
expose your vulnerable points. When you try to get your licks in
ahead of your opponent, you allow the initiative to pass to him. You
want to retain control of the situation at all times.

Although it might sound paradoxical, the best way to do this is to
let him state his side of the case first. Don't interrupt. Remember to
use the miracle people power tool of listening that I gave you back
in Chapter 5. It will work like magic for you.

If you interrupt the other person, you wound his ego and make
him feel unimportant. Not only that, you'll cause him to create a
mental block to what you say when it's your turn to talk. He simply
will not be willing to pay attention to you if you refuse to listen to
him first. So if you want him to hear your side of the case after he's
through speaking, then pay him the courtesy of listening to him.

"If a plan of mine runs into opposition, or if someone comes to me
with a complaint, I always make it a point to hear the person out,"
says Grace Ellison, Personnel Director for the U. S. Chemical Corporation. "What the individual says will usually give me a clue as
to how to proceed for he can expose the weaknesses in his argument
when he's talking.

"I even ask him to go over some of his main points again several
times and I continue to seek more information by asking him
whether there's anything else he wants to add.

"Before I state my side of the case, I do my best to show him I'm
keenly interested in his point of view. I let him do most of the
talking first, but I never let him take charge of the situation.
Actually, I retain control by keeping quiet, for he'll soon exhaust
himself from talking and then I can take over.

"If you want to be sure of winning every argument, always wait so you can have the final say-so. The person who talks first in any controversy inevitably defeats himself by talking too much."

It is an extremely good idea to get the person to repeat some of his key points or his sore spots when he comes to you all riled up, just as Ms. Ellison does. Letting him get it off his chest helps him immeasurably, but if you can get him to repeat his complaints to you several times, he literally drains himself emotionally.

It takes both mental and physical energy to argue with force. When he exhausts himself mentally and physically, it will be that much easier for you to win your argument by persuasion.

How to Probe and Explore His Argument

Unless the person is ready to receive a particular idea, he is not likely to accept it. You should lead him on an objective fact-finding survey of his position until you find a weakness in his argument.

When you find such a weakness, you can then use it for your opening argument to persuade him to your point of view. When he sees the weakness in his own argument, he will become much more receptive to your proposition.

You see, when you're trying to persuade someone to change his mind, it's better that you ask him to first justify his own position. If you know, for instance, that your position is stronger and more logical than his, weaknesses are bound to crop up as he talks. You can then use these weaknesses to penetrate his defenses.

How do you get him to state his viewpoint? By asking leading questions just as I showed you how to do back in Chapter 2. Let me give you a practical example that will show you how to make this technique work:

Dwight Farmer is a wholesale salesman who calls on retailers of automotive parts and accessories. "I don't try to sell the prospect on the benefits of buying my product right off the bat," Dwight says. "Instead, I ask him all about the items he's now selling. I ask questions like *how well does it hold up . . . how much trouble has it given him . . . whether he's had customer complaints or not . . . what kind of delivery service he's getting from the wholesaler . . .* that sort of thing.

"Somewhere he's bound to have a complaint of some sort about the current product he's handling. That gives me the opportunity to explore that area of weakness so I can show him how I can do a better job for him than the other fellow."

How can you yourself use this kind of approach? Suppose you want to persuade an employee to change his way of doing a particular job. You suggest the new method, but your employee insists that the old way is better. Now since you are the boss, you could put your foot down and demand that he change his work methods, or you can ask him to tell you why his way is better than yours.

By letting him state his argument first, you can get his ideas out into the open where you can probe them for weaknesses. The moment your employee realizes there are some holes in his case, he will be much more willing to accept your point of view. Persuasion is always better than force, even when you're the boss.

And if by some strange chance, his argument is sounder than yours, you can keep right on using the old methods instead of changing over to the new ones. Either way, you'll still win. This technique, by the way, will work on everyone.

How to Know When to Take Action

It's no use for you to take any positive action until you know the person is receptive to change. Weaknesses in a person's argument and his willingness to listen to your ideas will often be expressed either by statements of doubt or by questions.

For example, suppose you hear comments like this:

> "This is the way I see it, but I could be wrong on a point or two."

> "I'm always willing to listen to reason."

> "I've never looked at it that way before."

> "It's just possible I could be in error on this one small detail."

> "Well, we all make mistakes once in a while."

When you hear expressions of self-doubt like this, you know it's time for you to take over and present your arguments for the person is now receptive to change. He's ready to listen and be persuaded to your point of view.

Another clue to a person's willingness to change his mind can be detected by his use of questions. Such question words as *who, when, where, what, why,* and *how* are dead giveaways that the person is ready to change his mind, for he's asking for more information so he can make a decision that is favorable to you. Here are some examples of that:

"*Why* should I buy this from you?"

"*Why* do I have to do it this way?"

"*Where* can I get service if I switch to your product?"

"*Who* would be calling on me in the future?"

"*What* would be the advantages of my doing it this way?"

"*How* would this procedure benefit me?"

When you hear expressions of self-doubt or questions similar to these asking for more specific information, it's a clear signal to you that it's time for you to take action and present your side of the case.

How to State Your Side of the Argument

The tendency is always there to use the old forceful methods to win an argument. You'll have to discipline yourself to avoid this bad habit of trying to beat the other fellow down or to show him up. Even if you out-talk him to the point he isn't able to say anything at all in rebuttal, *you still will not win until he accepts your viewpoint as his very own or until he becomes willing to act on your idea.*

It's a proven fact psychologically that the best way to state your case is to do so moderately, accurately, and with deep sincerity. Be enthusiastic, by all means, but don't let your enthusiasm carry you away emotionally to the point where you exaggerate or make too forceful an approach.

An authority on this subject is Leonard A. Goodman, a professor with Washington University's Psychology Department. He feels this way about how to handle an argument or a conflict of opinions.

"The best way to change another person's mind so that he will be receptive to your ideas is to state your case fairly, accurately, and sincerely," Dr. Goodman says. "Ostentatious or flamboyant methods might be fine for high school debates where the speaker is graded by judges on delivery, style, grammar, vocabulary, enunciation, and so on, but they are no good to use anywhere else.

"In fact, if you use a debater's style of tearing down an opponent's case to win an argument, you'll lose every time. You cannot go at your listener with the slightest hint of criticism in your voice or an arrogant 'I'm absolutely right and you're completely wrong' attitude, and expect to win anything but his staunchest opposition."

You can use the "Yes, but . . ." technique to present your side of the case. When you use this approach, you soften your contradiction by seeming to agree with your listener like this:

"*Yes,* I understand what you mean, and I really agree with almost everything you say, Sam, *but* have you thought of this angle?"

When you use the "Yes, but . . ." technique, a person will listen to your idea good-naturedly and accept your suggestions more readily.

How to Use Witnesses to Win Your Case for You

Back in Chapter 12 I pointed out that the most important thing a trial lawyer can do in pleading his case is to bring on his witnesses to prove the points he wants to put across in court. He realizes that his argument will be much more convincing to the jury if disinterested people say a certain thing took place than if he himself says it.

The best salesman also uses testimonials of satisfied customers. That's how Jack Stone built his mail-order boot and shoe business up to more than a million dollars a year, remember? And politicians always fare better when they get other people to support them and blow their horn for them, too.

If you apply for a job, it's hard for you to praise yourself without appearing to be conceited and egotistical. But someone else can recommend you highly in a letter to your prospective employer and sound extremely convincing.

Just as important as human witnesses are records, statistics, documents, letters, quotations, examples, and so on that can be used as silent witnesses to prove your point so you can win your argument. Let me give you one practical for-instance.

Suppose you want to tap your boss for a raise. Don't say, "I think

I deserve a raise." That will usually get you nowhere. Instead, say, "My *record* will show that I've earned a raise."

So always use a third party when you can to fortify your position. Your listener will be much more inclined to pay attention to you when you do.

Don't Be Greedy

Most people who use force to argue try to prove the other person is completely and totally wrong on each and every point. They insist on winning 100 percent. This is a mistake. A skillful person, who uses persuasion rather than force, will always be willing to concede something to his opponent or give ground on some minor point.

So be flexible. Be willing to give ground, especially on some small detail. Compromise a little bit. Bend with the wind. You know the strong oak tree refuses to give in to the winds of a tropical typhoon as it roars across the islands of the Pacific so it is torn out by its roots to die. But the bamboo, slight of stature, and not nearly as strong and sturdy and as inflexible as the oak, bends with the wind and survives the wild carnage of nature. Do the same yourself and you'll survive, too.

When you know for sure you're going to win, when you know you're 100 percent right and the other person's all wrong, don't be greedy about it. Give in here and there on some small point. Just follow this rule and you'll be safe: *Give ground on trifles—never on principles.* All you need is the wisdom to know the difference between the two.

How to Help the Other Person Save Face

Not being greedy or insisting on winning your case 100 percent is one way you can help the other person save face. But that's only the beginning. You can do much more than that and here's how:

You see, many times in an argument a person realizes that he's wrong. He's already changed his mind and he'd like to agree with you openly, but unfortunately, that old ego in the form of false pride gets in the way. I know from my own personal experience that it's hard to admit you're wrong or that you've made a mistake, especially when you have taken a strong stand in public and committed yourself openly. If you find your opponent in that position, open the door for him. Help him find a way out of his dilemma.

One way you can do this is to suggest he might not have been aware of all the facts before he made up his mind. You might say, for instance, "John, did you have all the facts before you made up your mind? If you didn't know about this point, I can easily see why you made the decision you did. Under those circumstances I'd have done the same thing."

Even if John did have all the facts, he'll grab at this life line you've just thrown to him. All he need do is say he didn't have all the facts and he's out of his corner. You've achieved your goal. You've helped him to save face.

This method is especially valuable to use when you're dealing with anyone in a subordinate position, even a child. You point out the person's mistake so you can be sure he'll not do it again, but at the same time you save his feelings and keep from destroying his pride by saying you'd have done the same thing had you known only the facts he used to make his decision.

However you do it, the important thing is to help the person escape from his uncomfortable position. If you'll just remember that you should make friends—not enemies—whenever you win an argument, you'll be in fine shape. You'll be making good use of your miracle people power.

15

When All Else Fails, You Can Always Depend on This Technique to Miracle People Power

I'd like to start right off by making a strong and startling statement. *This method will work every time on everyone.* There are absolutely no exceptions. Out of every one thousand times at bat, you'll get one thousand hits. All you need do is follow the techniques you'll learn in this chapter.

But before we take up those techniques, I'd like to briefly review a couple of points with you. If you'll remember, back in Chapter 1, I told you about the twelve basic needs and desires every person has. Then in Chapter 2, I showed you how to help a person fulfill those basic needs and desires so you could in turn achieve miracle people power and get what you want.

Now the instructions I gave you in those first two chapters still hold true, of course. But if you're having a hard time figuring out what a person's most pressing desire is, or if you haven't been able to determine how to fulfill it for him, let me give you a helpful tip. *All you need do is make a person feel important, for you can always depend on his ego-hunger to help you get what you want.*

So the purpose of this chapter is to amplify and expand the information I gave you previously about this basic desire of every person to be important. I want to show you how to increase your own miracle people power by fulfilling a person's need for ego-gratification.

How Paul Meyer Used This Technique
to Become a Millionaire

Before Paul Meyer founded his world-famous Success Motivation Institute in Waco, Texas, he sold insurance in Florida. And had it not been for a flash of inspiration that came to him while keeping an insurance appointment at a yacht basin in Jacksonville, he might still be selling insurance.

But there were bigger things in store for Mr. Meyer. His sudden insight was to grow into a brand-new and different idea in packaging and selling success as a commodity—and Success Motivation Institute.

Mr. Meyer wisely reasoned that anyone who had a yacht must also have some good ideas on how to become successful. He jotted down the license numbers of those yacht club Cadillacs and Continentals, traced the owners, and then asked each one of them sincerely and honestly, to what they attributed their success.

Those wealthy people were deeply impressed with Mr. Meyer's sincere approach; they answered his questions openly without reservation. Mr. Meyer was practicing right there the technique you're learning in this chapter—*how to make another person feel important*. That's why he was able to get what he wanted, too: the answers to his questions.

You see, every single person in the world wants to be important. Every individual is an egotist, whether he likes to admit that or not. Every human being wants the approval and the attention of others. In spite of all their money, those wealthy people still craved attention. They still needed to be important.

Perhaps it is hard for you to understand why a millionaire, who seemingly has everything in the world that he needs or desires, still needs the approval and the attention of others. But it is true, for every person everywhere, rich or poor, wants and needs to be important in some way.

Those rich people drove Cadillacs and Continentals. They had yachts, mansions, and everything else imaginable that money could possibly buy. But they needed the one thing their money could not buy for them: *sincere attention—ego-gratification—a real feeling of importance.* Mr. Meyer gave them what they needed and wanted.

When he did, he got what he wanted in return: valuable information. He took their answers, sifted them, expanded them, and reassembled them along with some original concepts of his own. The end result became his own personal "Blueprint for Success" and the foundation for Success Motivation Institute's first course.

Today, SMI is the world's leading producer of personal motivation, supervision, leadership development, executive and management courses. And Paul Meyer is a millionaire many times over all because he knew how to use this step to miracle people power. He made the other person feel important so he could get what he wanted. You can do the same thing.

HOW YOU CAN BENEFIT FROM EVERY PERSON'S DESIRE TO BE IMPORTANT

You can always benefit and achieve miracle people power for yourself from a person's desire to be important. Do your best to fulfill that basic desire every person has. In a great many instances, you'll find that the need for ego-gratification is a person's most dominant desire. But whether it is or not, you will never go wrong by making a man or a woman important or by feeding their ego. Make it a habit and a regular routine to do this for every single person with whom you come in contact. You'll always achieve more miracle people power when you do.

Perhaps you've heard this idea before. Could be you've been told many times that people want to be important, that they need to be heard and recognized, that they demand attention. But do you really know how to make another person feel more important? Do you know how to fulfill this craving for ego-gratification?

You see, just knowing that a person wants to be important is not nearly enough. You must show him how he can get what he wants. You must know how to gratify and feed his ego before you can ever hope to gain miracle people power so you can get what you want, too. This step will show you exactly how to do that.

TECHNIQUES YOU CAN USE TO GAIN THE BENEFITS

How to Make Every Single Person Feel More Important

> "No one pays any attention to me . . . no one ever listens to my ideas . . . nobody's interested in my opinion . . . they just want to do things their own way. . . ."

Ever hear comments like these before? Ever make the same remarks yourself? If you've ever felt this way, then you should be able to easily understand that other people feel the same way, too.

You can make a person feel important by paying attention to him . . . by asking for his opinions and ideas. When you do that, then listen—*really listen*—with rapt attention to what he has to say. To do so proves to him that you feel that what he has to tell you is important, that you respect his opinion, that you feel he has something worthwhile to offer.

> "When you ask a person for his ideas and opinions, you let him know he's both needed and wanted in your company," says Dale Walters, president of the Walters Supply Company, a wholesaler for the building trades in Omaha, Nebraska. "No one wants to be a non-entity or just another clock-number on the payroll. Every single person in your organization wants to be an important member of your team. Everyone wants to feel that he belongs where he is.
>
> "Ask your employees for their advice and their help and you will give them that individual identity they want and need so much. You make them valuable members of your team when you do this. They will work that much harder for you when they feel that they're making a major contribution to the success of your organization."

There are few faster ways to miracle people power than to ask a person for his valuable opinion, advice, or help. Do this and you will automatically make a person feel more important. And you'll increase your miracle people power, too.

If You're the Boss, Do This

If you're the boss, an excellent way to make your people feel important is to keep your door open to them. Such a policy will let your employees know that you're interested in them. They will feel they have access to you, that they can reach you, talk with you, tell you their ideas, give you their opinions, bring you their grievances and problems—and that you will listen to them.

But if you close your door to your people, if you isolate yourself from them, you let them know by your attitude and your actions that you're not interested in them and that you do not consider them important at all. You do not need to say anything; your closed door will say it quite plainly enough for you.

John De Butts, Chairman of the Board of the American Telephone and Telegraph Company, says that the open door policy has been a major factor in his successful business career.

I, myself, am convinced that you must keep the door of your mind open to others in all your relationships with people if you are going to make them feel important. Take your own son or daughter, for instance. If you won't listen to them, if you won't at least expose yourself to their ideas and their opinions, how can you make them feel important and valuable to you? The same can be said for your relationships with your husband, your wife, your friends. So keep the door of your mind open to others. You'll achieve much miracle people power when you do.

You Can Always Make a Person
Feel More Important by Doing This

Another fast and dependable way to make a person feel more important is to give him more responsibility. If at all possible, make him the boss . . . put him in charge *even if he has no one to supervise.*

I can still recall, although it's been many years ago, when a rubber factory employee named Bill was giving the management fits. Bill felt he'd been cheated at one time by the company so he was doing everything possible to make life miserable for his section supervisor, his department foreman, and management in general.

He would prolong his coffee breaks, turn out shoddy production, cheat on his incentive report sheet, clock in late and leave early. He was the leader of a team of six employees and as Bill went, so went the team.

Bill was not in my department, but I watched this battle of wits with great interest. Every possible effort was made by the supervisor and foreman to find a solution to the problem. Nothing seemed to work. And Bill couldn't be fired; he was too smart for that. Time and again management tried to get rid of him—only to lose the case when it went before the arbitration board.

Then one day I watched a safety drill. I noticed how Bill immediately took over and assumed command in the absence of his supervisor even though it was not his appointed job to do so. "Why not give Bill the responsibility for safety in that section?" I said to the supervisor and foreman. "Make him responsible and see what happens."

With much reluctance and misgiving, they did as I suggested. The results were absolutely astounding. Bill now had responsibility and he acted accordingly. He didn't want to lose his new-found authority and almost overnight he became a model employee simply because management had recognized his hungry ego and made him feel important as an individual.

Will this method always work? Read the following two examples and judge for yourself. Indiana Bell Telephone used to assemble its telephone books in 21 steps—each one performed by a different clerk. Now it gives each clerk the individual responsibility for putting an entire book together. As a result, less mistakes occur in the assembly process. Employee turnover has been reduced more than 50 percent.

Kaiser Steel was ready to close a continuous-weld pipe mill in California because they could not compete with Japanese prices. One hundred and fifty workers would lose their jobs. Labor asked management to let them have the full responsibility for making their product competitive with the Japanese. Management agreed and the workers put their heads to work.

They overhauled some tools, rearranged the production flow to make it more efficient, and made some changes in scheduling. The result? Production went up one-third, waste dropped from 20 percent down to 9 percent, and they were able to keep the plant open.

You can also look back at Chapter 6 for even more examples of the success to be gained when you make a person feel more important by giving him more responsibility. You see, when you give a person more responsibility, you must also grant him more authority to make decisions. That makes him feel more valuable as an individual.

How to Know What's Important to Every Person

If you are still at a loss as to how to make a person feel more important, let me give you a little tip. You'll always be right if you *talk to a man about himself . . . his children . . . his property or his personal possessions*. You can always make him feel more important by discussing one of these subjects with him and here's why:

People Always Like to Talk About Themselves

"People are basically selfish," says Dr. Edwin Barnes, a Los Angeles psychiatrist. "They are chiefly interested in themselves. They don't really care whether the government owns the railroads or whether the aircraft industry gets a subsidy or not—unless it's going to hit them in the pocketbook. Then they become vitally interested for it's going to affect them financially."

There is nothing more interesting to a man than himself sums up quite well what Dr. Barnes is saying here. You can put this idea to work for yourself by making sure your product, your service, or your conversation conforms to this fundamental characteristic of human nature.

People always feel more important when you tell them how handsome they are, how smart they are, how reliable and honest, what wise decisions they make, and so on.

If you want to gain more miracle people power for yourself, all you need do is forget your own needs and desires and talk to a person about how important he is. Do that; you're bound to succeed.

People Also Like to Talk About Their Children

Next to themselves, people like to talk about their children. They want to let you know how pretty little Jenna is, how smart young Bill is, what a fine football player Tim will be, how Sally has the voice to become a brilliant recording artist.

How many deadly dull and boring children's church or school programs have you sat through just so you could see and hear your own child perform? Why is it you're far less interested in the football game when your son is sitting on the bench?

We relive our own lives again in the lives of our children. We try to make them successful where we failed. Our own egos are fed when they do whatever we wanted to do, or when people compliment us for the achievements of our sons and daughters.

You can take full advantage of this human trait to attain more miracle people power for yourself. You can be sure that when you ask a person about his children and their accomplishments, you'll make him feel more important. You'll feed his hungry ego.

People Like to Talk About Their Property and Personal Possessions

Tell a man what a wise decision he made in buying such a beautiful house in the country; he'll be your friend. Tell his wife how exquisite her taste is in her choice of furniture; she'll love you for it.

Everyone wants to hear how wise they were in buying their house, their furniture, the car, the boat, even the golf clubs, and so on. You make people feel more important when you tell them how smart they are.

"When you tell a man how good-looking his house, his car, or his furniture is, you're really complimenting his good judgment," says Doctor Frank Cameron, a clinical psychologist from Tulsa, Oklahoma. "You make him feel important when you do that. You're letting him know how wise he was to make such intelligent decisions."

How to Make Everybody Feel Like Somebody

Sportswriters often ask Eddie Robinson, head football coach at Grambling College, how he can win so many football games year after year.

Mr. Robinson's answer is that he tries to make everybody feel like somebody. He treats every player as an important individual, not just as a cog in a machine. If a player thinks he can make it as a fullback, he gets the chance to prove it. If he makes it, fine. If not, at least he knows his coach thought enough of him as a person to give him the opportunity.

But it wasn't always that way. In the beginning Robinson handled his players like robots. He switched them around constantly without ever once asking a player what his own desires were. As he puts it, "I was switching people around faster than a short order cook filling orders." But it didn't work; the team kept on losing.

Trying to find an answer, Robinson looked back to his own college days at Leland College in Baker, Louisiana. And he remembered his football coach, Ruben S. Turner, telling him, "Everybody is somebody."

That was the turning point. He put up a sign in the dressing room that said, EVERYBODY IS SOMEBODY, and he began treating his players that way. Grambling started winning and has been doing it ever since.

If you want to win with people, if you want to achieve more miracle people power for yourself, you can do the same. All you need do is *treat everybody like somebody*. You're bound to get results.

16

Miracle People Power Orders That Always Bring Miraculous Results

Although you might not be the big boss yet, still there'll be times when you need to tell other people specifically what to do. You think not? You say you don't have a job where you give instructions or issue orders to anyone at all? You never tell anyone else what to do? Funny thing. Could be just a coincidence, but you sound exactly like someone who tried to tell me the same story last week.

"I'm in no position to give orders to anyone . . . I'm only a house-wife . . . I don't have a job of any kind," Barbara Moore said. Yet less than an hour later, she was standing before a group of volunteer workers, telling them what their specific duties were going to be in the annual United Fund drive.

Why was Barbara doing that? Well, she'd been given the task of organizing and directing the collection activities for the entire south-west section of her city. Her area alone had a population of more than 50 thousand. But she never gave orders to anyone, she said.

So I know there will be times when you'll have to issue orders and give instructions to people, too. In this chapter, I want to show you how to use your miracle people power to get the results you want when you tell others what to do.

I realize full well that not all action is initiated or accomplished by the use of orders. Many times you can get a great deal done just by using suggestions, making requests, or asking questions.

But when the circumstances call for an order, I want you to be able to issue one in a positive and confident manner, stating clearly and precisely who is to do what, when and where. That's the whole purpose of this chapter.

BENEFITS YOU'LL GAIN

1. People will respond quickly to orders and directives that are concise, clear, and easy to understand.
2. Your group will be motivated to work more effectively when they know exactly what their jobs are and when they know precisely what you want them to do.
3. When you issue orders that are simple to understand and easy to carry out, you can decentralize the work more effectively.
4. Proper orders will eliminate waste, confusion, and duplication of effort. People will do what you want done, and they'll do it right the first time.
5. If you issue the correct orders to others, they'll not have to come back time and again for clarification of what you said. You'll have more time to get your own work done.

TECHNIQUES YOU CAN USE TO GAIN THE BENEFITS

How to Know When to Issue an Order

It isn't always necessary to issue an order to get things going. Certain details in our daily lives or our work are so routine they almost handle themselves. For instance, you don't need to give your wife instructions to cook dinner, nor do you need to issue orders to your people at the end of the day to come back to work the next morning.

Nor do you need to issue an order to prove you're the boss. If you're in charge of a department or section, your people know that already. You don't have to prove that point to them by issuing some unnecessary order. Let me give you an example to show you exactly what I mean by that.

I'd been called in as a management consultant to help a particular tire and rubber company solve their low morale problem. It was especially bad in one department. One morning I stood with that young department foreman watching the changeover of shifts.

It was just short of seven A.M. The day shift had already reported in. They stood by their machinery waiting to be told by their supervisor about the day's production schedule. They needed only his word to start things rolling.

The night shift was finished, but they couldn't clock out until seven. They were bone-tired, for they'd been on their feet all through the night. Now that their work was finished, they squatted down on their haunches to rest, or sat on stacks of rubber skids out of the way just waiting for the seven o'clock whistle to blow.

That was the system in the plant; the men were not violating any order. But that morning the young department foreman had just been chewed out by the production superintendent. He was spoiling for a fight. He was looking for any excuse he could find to take out his anger on someone else so he could restore his injured pride and ego. He called the night supervisor over.

"Get your men up on their feet," he snapped. "I don't allow anyone to sit down while he's working in my department and you know that. I'm not running a damned rest home here."

"But Bart, my men are all through," the night supervisor said. "You know we have a ten minute shift changeover period. They're not actually on duty now. They're just waiting for the seven o'clock whistle to blow."

"Don't talk back to me," the foreman yelled. "I'm the boss in this department and don't you ever forget it. Your men are still on the clock so get 'em on their feet. That's an order, damn it!"

The point is, if you're the boss, your people already know that. You don't have to issue them an order to prove it. But if you do need to issue an order to get the job done, then by all means, do so. Don't be afraid of hurting someone's feelings by telling him what to do. If that's your job and it has to be done, then do it.

How to Make Sure You Actually Need to Issue an Order

As a result of long experience in business and management, I've found that an order is needed in only four specific situations:

1. To initiate some action.
2. To correct a mistake or solve a problem in the action.
3. To speed up or slow down the action.
4. To stop the action.

Could be you'll come up with some other situation where you feel you need to issue an order. If that's the case, fine; just add yours to my list. And do me a favor, will you? Let me know if you do.

Use Your Established Line of Authority to Issue Your Orders

In the armed services, it's called *chain of command.* In companies and corporations it's usually known as the *organizational line of authority.* No matter what it's called, and regardless of how large or small the group is, it always has a definite fixed chain of command or line of authority through which orders, commands, instructions, and suggestions are channeled. If a group doesn't have that line of authority established, then it's not an organization after all—it's only a bunch or a mob, in spite of its title.

It is absolutely essential that you use this authority line when you issue your orders. If secondary supervisors are bypassed, they will lose their authority in the eyes of their own subordinates. They could react by becoming recalcitrant leaders of dissident groups and even try to undermine you in an effort to regain their lost status.

To bypass the supervisor below you is not only a violation of good management procedure, but it can also be confusing to an employee, especially if the order you give him disagrees with the one he's received previously from his immediate superior. *No man can serve two masters,* Jesus said, and that is as true today as it was when He first said it nearly two thousand years ago.

Even though you use your established line of authority to issue your orders, this will not keep you from picking a certain person to do a specific job.

Suppose you know in your own mind that Brown is the best man for the special task that's to be done. Just tell his supervisor why you want Brown to do the job. That should be the end of it unless that supervisor knows of some good reason why Brown should not do it.

How to Issue Clear, Concise, and Positive Orders: A Check-List

First, I'd like to list six basic points you can use to check yourself out to be sure you're issuing a clear, concise, and positive order. Then I'll discuss each one of them with you briefly.

1. Be sure you know what you want first.
2. Concentrate on a single objective.
3. Prepare your order in your mind or in writing.
4. Issue the appropriate order.
5. Make your order fit the person.
6. Use mission-type orders whenever you can.

Be Sure You Know What You Want First

It's absolutely essential that you know precisely the results you're after before you tell anyone to do anything. Too many orders grow like a rambling rose, creeping ivy, or the crabgrass in my yard.

Incomplete, vague, and ambiguous orders will get you the same kind of results. If you are not sure of what you want, then you're not yet ready to issue an order.

To help you determine the results you're after, follow these seven simple guidelines so you can use the same thinking pattern each time you issue an order.

1. *What* exactly is it that I want to accomplish?
2. *Who* is the best person to do this job?
3. *When* does the work have to be completed?
4. *Why* is the job necessary?

5. *Where* is the best location for the work to be done?
6. *How* will the job be done?
7. *How much* will it cost?

By following these seven points, you'll box yourself into a corner and be forced to answer such relevant questions as *what, who, when, why, where, how,* and *how much.* You're bound to improve your ability to issue orders when you do this. And another happy end result will be that your ability to insure that the job is understood, supervised, and accomplished will also improve.

Concentrate on a Single Objective

Even though there might be a great number of details to be taken care of in your order, these will all fall into place quite naturally if your order has but one specific final objective. So don't clutter up your mind with a mass of trivia that confuses you or clouds the main issue. Keep it simple. Let your subordinates work out the details of your plan. That's what they should be paid for.

Prepare Your Order in Your Mind or in Writing

A great many orders are issued orally on the spot to correct a mistake. If you see something wrong, I'm sure you're not about to rush back to your office to dictate a long directive to your secretary. I feel certain you'll correct the error right then and there.

How to know, then, when to issue an order verbally or when to put it in writing? Or, how to know when to issue an order verbally and follow it up in writing? Colonel Robert Fairchild, a veteran of more than 25 years of military service, says this about that question.

"If your order is going to change established policy or procedure, then it has to be in writing, no matter how simple it is. An oral order should be used primarily to correct a basic mistake the person is making. If that oral order changes an existing policy, then it has to be confirmed in writing as soon as possible to prevent any confusion or possible misunderstanding."

That is a good rule of thumb to follow. Besides that, though, I would like to say that if your order covers more than three major points, put it in writing. Then you'll not run the risk of being misunderstood.

Issue the Appropriate Order

You don't need a ten page memorandum to say "Fire! Everybody out!" But if you're working in a scientific or research lab with dangerous chemicals, a carefully written, step-by-step plan is a must.

But don't confuse all your previous detailed plans with the final order you give either. For instance, the written documents that were prepared for the invasion of Normandy in World War II would completely fill a room of more than 200 cubic feet. Yet General Eisenhower kicked off that huge operation with a simple 23 word sentence that said, "You will enter the continent of Europe and undertake operations aimed at the heart of Germany and the destruction of her armed forces."

My point is that you should issue your actual order at the working level in as few simple words as humanly possible.

Make Your Order Fit the Person

The experience, background, education, intelligence, and position of the person who's receiving your order will all play a great part in how you word what you say in your order.

However, even the most educated person will be happy to get his instructions in the simplest words possible. Your best bet is to use the clearest, most concise language you can to avoid mistakes and misunderstanding. If you must use technical or scientific terms to make your point, do so, but surround those words with simple ones like *make, work, do, push, pull.* You'll get your message across then with no trouble at all.

Use Mission-Type Orders Whenever You Can

Simply said, a mission-type order tells a person what you want done, but it doesn't tell him how to do it. The how-to is left entirely up to the person who's going to carry out your order.

When you use mission-type orders, you emphasize skill—not rules. Your subordinates will be challenged to use their initiative, imagination, and resourcefulness to get the job done. You'll bring out the best in them.

Mission-type orders will also bring out the worst in others. They will help you weed out incompetent individuals faster than any other method I know of. You don't have to fire such people. They will literally eliminate themselves for they simply can't keep up.

How to Check for Understanding

When you issue an order, it's not only important that you make yourself completely understood, but it's also just as important that you word your order so it cannot possibly be misunderstood.

You can do three specific things to determine whether you've been misunderstood or not. Use them all every time you issue an order if you want to prevent any misunderstandings or mistakes.

1. Encourage your people to ask you questions.
2. Ask them questions yourself to check their understanding.
3. Have them repeat your oral instructions.

Most people have no trouble at all with the first two, but they tend to stumble over the last one. They're always so afraid they might hurt someone's feelings by asking them to repeat their orders.

You don't have to worry about that. There's a very simple way out. All you need do is say, "Would you mind repeating what I've just said? I want to double-check *myself* to make sure *I* didn't leave anything out, or that *I* didn't say the wrong thing."

How to Check for Progress

No order is ever complete unless you supervise its execution. You must use thought and care in your supervision. Over-supervision stifles initiative and creates resentment; under-supervision will not get the job done for you.

To supervise the execution of your orders without harassing your people, use the following system:

A SEVEN POINT FAIL-SAFE INSPECTION PROCEDURE

1. **Set Up a Definite Amount of Time for Daily Inspections.** Always inspect some phase of your operation every day. Never let a day go by without doing so. Allocate a specific number of minutes or hours for your inspection in your work schedule.

2. **Go Over Your Inspection Points Before You Inspect.** Study up and review your selected points before you inspect. That way you won't be caught short. No one will ever be able to make a fool out of you. Check no less than three, but no more than eight, specific points on any one inspection.

3. **Inspect Only the Points You Select.** Cover only the points you've selected to insepct. Don't look at the ones your people are trying to show you. This can become a cat and mouse game if you let it get away from you. Remember who's inspecting and who's being inspected. When you're the boss, you must retain control at all times.

4. **Always Bypass Your Line of Authority.** When you issue an order, always use your line of authority. *When you inspect, never use your line of authority.* No other kind of inspection is ever satisfactory. You should take the immediate supervisor along when you inspect, but don't ask him questions. Question the man who's actually doing the job.

5. **Ask Questions and More Questions.** The best way to get accurate information about your operation is to ask questions. Don't ask questions that can be answered *yes* or *no* unless you follow them up with *why* or *what for*.

6. **Re-Check the Mistakes You Find.** An inspection is worthless unless you correct the mistakes you find. So follow up. Reinspect. Supervise and make certain your corrective orders are carried out.

7. **Vary Your Supervisory Routine.** If you inspect every morn-

ing at eight A.M., soon your inspection will be of no value. So vary your schedule. Never do the same thing the same way twice in a row. Inspect when your people least expect it. If you have a 24 hour around-the-clock operation, don't forget to inspect the graveyard shift, too.

How to Issue Your Orders
so People Will Want to Carry Them Out

The words in your order tell what is to be done. The way you say it will determine how it will be done. To get the best out of your people, follow these simple guidelines:

1. Disguise your orders as suggestions or requests.
2. Never issue an order you can't enforce.
3. Indicate by your manner you expect immediate compliance.
4. Show faith in a person's abilities to do the job.

What to Do When Things Go Wrong

I know it's hard to admit it when you've made a mistake, but it's extremely wise to do so. Don't let false pride get in your way. When you're wrong, stop—back up—and start all over. Things will get better right away when you do.

17

How Miracle People Power Can Actually Make Others Welcome Your Criticism

At first glance, you might feel you don't have to criticize or correct the actions of other people, but if you'll take an honest look at your daily activities, you'll soon find that you do. If you are a department manager, a section supervisor, a plant superintendent, a businessman or woman, an executive of any sort, I'm sure that hardly a day goes by that you don't have to call attention to someone's mistakes. That being so, I know you can definitely use the *Miracle People Power Check-List for Formal Criticism* that's in this chapter to your own advantage.

First of all, I think we ought to be sure we're both using the same language. What is criticism anyway? Well, the dictionary definition starts right off by saying that criticism is disapproval or fault-finding. I personally feel that criticism is what we usually say about other people who don't have the same faults that we have.

What is a critic then? The dictionary says a critic is a person who makes judgments of the merits and faults of books, music, pictures, plays, acting, and so on. It also says that a critic is a person whose profession is writing judgments for a newspaper or a magazine. And finally, the dictionary says a critic is a person who disapproves or finds fault; a fault-finder.

Now when it comes to being a critic or using criticism to get the job done, I feel much as Josh Billings did when he said, "To be a good critic demands more brains than most men possess." I feel I can get much better and far longer lasting results with praise and appreciation than I could ever hope to attain with criticism.

No one likes to be criticized. No one wants to be told that he is wrong. Criticism has the potential power to destroy a person. It is one of man's deadliest weapons. Unless a person has a completely sadistic outlook on life, he does not enjoy finding fault with another individual or criticizing him.

You might ask, then, why did I write this chapter? Why did I include it in this book? Well, unfortunately, there will be times when you have no other choice than to criticize. There'll be no other way out. Sometimes not to criticize, to overlook a mistake, is far worse than to discipline or to punish the person. And criticism is a form of punishment without a doubt. So you might as well accept the idea that at times you will have to reprimand, you'll have to criticize, and you'll have to punish others.

But you don't have to destroy a person when you criticize him. You can offer him advice, counsel, and guidance in such a way that he'll scarcely realize you're finding fault with him. That's the purpose of this chapter: to show you how to use your miracle people power so effectively that others will actually welcome your criticism. I want to show you how to criticize and say it with flowers. When you use the techniques you'll learn in this chapter—

YOU'LL GAIN THESE BENEFITS

1. You'll eliminate certain bad habits and undesirable behavior of people.
2. People will do a better job for you. They won't make the same mistake twice in a row.
3. Individual and group discipline and morale will both improve.
4. You'll get far better results from all your people, even those you don't criticize.

5. Production, performance, and profits will all increase and improve because things will get done right the first time.

TECHNIQUES YOU CAN USE TO GAIN THESE BENEFITS

How to Avoid This Major Stumbling Block

As I said a moment ago, criticism is what we usually say about other people who don't have the same faults that we have. This can be a major stumbling block for you if you don't watch out.

You see, most of the time when we tell another person all about the terrible bad habits he has, we're not really trying to help him at all. We're telling him all this so we can build up ourselves by tearing him down.

If you want to avoid this major obstacle to good human relationships, just ask yourself if you're really trying to help the other person in some way. Are you honestly trying to aid him? How? Why? Or are you only trying to increase your own feeling of superiority by belittling him?

What are some of the clues you can watch for? Well, if you hear yourself saying, "I'm telling you this for your own good," or "I wouldn't tell you this if I didn't think so much of you," or "If I were you . . .," watch out. I doubt very much if you're really trying to help the other individual at all. I'd be inclined to guess that your main purpose is to justify your own mistakes by making his seem much worse.

"This is the old shell game," Art W., a recovered alcoholic and a member of Alcoholics Anonymous for 12 years, says. "You know, when I was drinking I had to get the spotlight off myself by pointing out the moral defects of other people. I'd say I wasn't so bad after all. I didn't gamble like so and so, or I didn't sleep with other women, that sort of thing. That's the only way a drunk can retain any semblance whatever of his self-esteem, by calling attention to other people's faults and shortcomings."

If you've been guilty of action like this, and who hasn't, don't feel bad. You're in the majority. But you can change, too.

How to Correct a Mistake Without Formal Criticism

Now that you know when *not* to criticize, let's find out when you should criticize. Or better yet, let's find out *why* you should criticize. Your primary purpose should be to gain the benefits I've already mentioned. If by criticizing, you'll be able to correct certain bad habits and change the undesirable behavior of the people who work for you, then you should criticize them. If people will do a better job for you, if discipline and morale will improve, if you'll get better all-around results, if production, performance, and profits all increase, then you can feel well justified in using criticism to get the job done.

But many times you will not need to hold a formal counseling session with a person to get him to improve his performance. On-the-spot corrections without name calling can often do the trick for you. If you can get the improvement you want without resorting to formal criticism of a specific individual, so much the better.

"Direct, formal, face-to-face criticism should be used only as a last resort," says Bruce Holloway, a department supervisor with the Black and Decker Power Tool Manufacturing Company. "For instance, when I see that something's gone haywire in my department, I don't go looking for a culprit or a scapegoat. I simply want to find out what happened or what went wrong. I'm searching for facts.

"If I can correct the mistake, whatever it is, without using any specific names in front of the group, I will. I'm more interested in performance than I am in punishment. I've also found that the responsible party, whoever he is, will be so darned grateful that I didn't pinpoint him in front of everybody, he'll never make that same mistake again.

"This method works 95 percent of the time. I get what I want without cutting down any one individual. Mistakes are corrected; they don't happen again. On-the-job efficiency goes up; worker morale and discipline are better. All in all, performance, production, and profits increase and improve. These are the results we want."

I'm sure those are the benefits and the results that you want for yourself, too. And you can gain them if you remember to bear down on the mistake and not on the personality. I know it's sometimes a great temptation to take the easy way out and call someone *stupid, dumb, lazy, careless,* and so on. But in the long run it's not the easy way out, so don't do it. Just focus down on the act that you're criticizing—not on the person.

When, Where, and How to Use Direct and Formal Criticism

Direct and formal criticism should be used only when it is the last possible way to get the job done. If you can get mistakes corrected by using the previous technique, then by all means, do so.

But if you cannot, then chances are you'll have no choice but to take someone to task for what he's done. Before you do that, though, make sure you get all the pertinent facts first. Get the whole truth of the matter before you start assigning blame for the mistake.

You can't get to the bottom of things unless your people know that you will accept the truth from them. They must realize that they can *tell the boss what he has to hear—not what he wants to hear,* and not be crucified for doing so.

What's the best way to dig out all the facts? That's right, by asking questions just as I told you to do back in Chapters 1 and 2. Use the question words *who, what, when, where, why, how,* and *how much* to get at the truth. And don't forget the phrase, *"Is there any other reason?"* You can use it to good advantage here.

When you do have all the facts at hand and when you know specifically the person you're going to criticize, work out your exact procedure before you call him in. Unless you criticize an individual with great wisdom and judgment, you can easily defeat your purpose.

How to go about this, then? Easy. Think back to what I told you about a person's basic needs and desires and how to use them to your own advantage. Then show him the benefits he's going to gain by doing as you ask him to do. Tell him about the advantages that will be his when he corrects his mistake. Always talk in terms of what he needs and what he wants. Then he'll listen to you—but not before.

To help you do this, I've made up a check-list you can use to correct a person's mistakes without offending him: 13 guidelines you can follow that will actually make an individual accept and welcome your criticism.

MIRACLE PEOPLE POWER CHECK-LIST
FOR FORMAL CRITICISM

1. Pick the correct time and place.
2. Criticize in complete privacy.
3. Never lose your temper.
4. Begin with sincere praise and appreciation.
5. Take your own inventory, too.
6. Criticize the act . . . not the person.
7. One mistake to an interview.
8. Be specific about the mistake to correct.
9. Let the other person tell his side of it, too.
10. Fit the punishment to the crime.
11. Ask for cooperation.
12. Emphasize the benefits to be gained.
13. Finish with sincere praise and appreciation.

Pick the Correct Time and Place

If you're criticizing a person by making an on-the-spot correction, then you should do so as soon as you see the mistake being made. This is direct criticism, but it could hardly be called formal. Corrections like these are most often made during an inspection or while actually supervising a man's work.

But if you are conducting a performance review of a man's work for the last six months or so, then you'd want to pick an appropriate time and place to get the maximum results that you're after.

Some managers think Friday afternoon is the best time for a heart-to-heart talk. I disagree. You run the risk of a person brooding all weekend over what you said and coming back to work the first of the week still sour about his chewing-out. Others prefer Monday morning, but I know from experience that's a bad time for no one's really into the swing of things yet for the week.

I personally like Tuesday morning. That way I can let a person know by a wave of the hand, a pat on the back, or a cheery "Hello" during the rest of the week that I carry no grudge.

If possible, hold your interview in a quiet place—your private office, if you have one. If you need to shout at a person to make yourself heard, there'll be a further chance for misunderstanding. Yell at a man and he could easily interpret noise for anger.

Criticize in Complete Privacy

Public criticism causes humiliation and deep resentment. It can be disastrous, for reprimands in the presence of others burn themselves deep into the mind, forming permanent scars that never can be erased.

To determine the exact results of public and private criticism on performance of duty, a team of Pentagon psychologists from the Department of the Army evaluated a company of 200 basic trainees at Fort Ord, California.

They divided the soldiers into 20 squads and gave each one the same set of difficult duties to perform. Then they critiqued each squad on its performance, but in different ways. Then they had them do the same jobs over again.

The army psychologists found that 75 percent of those criticized in private did better the next time. However, only 25 percent of those criticized in front of their fellow trainees improved their performance the second time around.

The lesson here is perfectly clear: if you want to get the best results out of your criticism, be sure to keep it completely private.

Never Lose Your Temper

It's best never to lose your temper with a person who works for you. But above all, never do so in a counseling session. If you do, you will end up with nothing more than a hot-tempered argument between two angry people. Chances are neither one of you will be able to remember the point of the interview.

If you can't see any other good results except for your temporarily feeling better for having blown off steam, don't do it. You're a human being, not a radiator. Don't let personal feelings and personal opinions creep into your daily work. That's the "Jones, you ought to part your hair on the other side" kind of criticism. It's absolutely useless.

That kind of criticism will go in one ear and out the other—if you're lucky. If the person remembers any of it at all, he'll only recall that you lost your temper, that you were sarcastic, or that you criticized him unjustly when he didn't really have it coming.

Begin with Sincere Praise and Appreciation

Don't tear a man apart the moment he comes into your office. Nor should you enumerate all his defects of character one after another as if you were ticking off a grocery list. No one lives who can take that kind of punishment for very long.

Instead, tell a person how good he is, how much you think of him, what a good job he's done, *all except for this one small point that you want to discuss with him*.

Kind words help establish a friendly, cooperative atmosphere. Praise and compliments open the other person's mind. You can use comments like these to make him receptive to your criticism:

"Tom, that was certainly a fine progress report you made. You definitely covered all the main points. However, there is just one thing I do want to take up with you. . . ."

"Annie, you've done excellent work for me. However, there is one idea for self-improvement I'd like to discuss with you. . . ."

"Hank, I know you're always looking for new ways to improve your work procedures. I've noted one thing you're doing that seems to be causing you a problem so I'd like to suggest. . . ."

Take Your Own Inventory, Too

A good way to take some of the sting out of your criticism is to let the person know you're not infallible. This helps him to better accept your comments. Bert Johnson, a department foreman with the 3 M Corporation, does it this way.

"I start off by telling a person how I've done a similar thing before myself," Bert says. "Then I tell him what I did to correct my own mistake. The average man identifies with me, gets my point at once, and there are no hard feelings about it either."

I've used the same system myself for many years. It works extremely well with everyone, even young people. I recommend it highly.

Criticize the Act . . . Not the Person

When you criticize a person, it's important that you not destroy his dignity. Let him save face. The best way to do this is never to criticize him, but to criticize what he did. Look at these examples and you'll see immediately what I mean by that.

RIGHT: This word is misspelled.
WRONG: Miss Smith, your typing is terrible.

RIGHT: Sam, please check the measurements on this.
WRONG: Of all the idiotic stupid things to do . . .

RIGHT: Tom, if you want to get an A, you must study harder.
WRONG: Why do you bring home such dumb report cards?

Note that whenever you criticize the person instead of the act, you tend to use sarcasm and ridicule. Words like *stupid, dumb, lazy,* and *idiot* tend to creep into the conversation.

This is not an effective method of correction as those Department of Army psychologists from the Pentagon discovered. They found that when they used sarcasm and ridicule to criticize the basic trainees rather than criticizing their mistakes, improvement on the second performance dropped down to rock bottom—less than 10 percent.

One Mistake to an Interview

A tendency most people have during a formal interview or counseling session is to overload the person with every mistake they can think of since he's been working for them.

For instance, you call a person in to point out *one* mistake. He agrees with you and seems willing to cooperate, so you decide to give him the whole load as long as you've got him on the run. You even bring up mistakes he's already corrected that should have been forgotten long ago. When you criticize a person, you should never bring up a mistake unless it has *not* been corrected.

Too much criticism at one time is extremely destructive. Your subordinate will become bitter and resentful. He'll feel that you're picking on him or nagging at him.

So stick to only one point at a time. Next week or next month, when he's solved his most pressing current problem, talk to him about something else that's bothering you. Maybe by that time, it might no longer be as big a sore spot as it is right now.

Be Specific About the Mistake to Correct

Criticism, to be effective and constructive, must be concrete and specific. The person must know exactly what he is doing wrong and how he can correct his mistake. Your whole interview can be wasted if you don't let the person know exactly what he can do to improve his performance. That's the purpose of the whole exercise, remember? So help supply his answer.

Vague statements such as "You don't have the proper attitude . . . You ought to be more careful . . . That's not right at all . . . You need to act differently . . ." are all completely useless by themselves alone. You should give specific instructions of what is to be done and why.

For instance, I can recall the time my son, Bob, came home from his high school shop class all in a huff. He insisted he was going to drop out. Finally we got the whole story from him.

His instructor had criticized a project he was working on by saying, "Oh, Bob, that's no good at all." But he didn't follow through with any concrete suggestions about how to make things right. So Bob was crushed. Not only was his work wrong, but now he didn't know how to correct his mistakes.

If you want to get the most mileage out of your criticism, be specific about the error to be corrected. Tell the person exactly what he is doing that is wrong and show him how he can correct his

mistake. Most people are anxious to do the right thing when they
know what the right thing is.

Let the Other Person Tell His Side of It, Too

Give the person plenty of opportunity to present his viewpoint,
too. Most people are extremely anxious to let you know exactly
what happened and how. They want to make sure you understand
and most of them will talk readily if you just give them the chance.

If a person does seem reluctant to speak up, ask him some leading
questions. Keep asking *why . . . why . . . why*. When you get
all the answers from him, you'll be in a much better position to
help him—and yourself, too, for that matter—by taking the appropriate action to keep this same mistake from happening again.

Fit the Punishment to the Crime

Before you mete out punishment for the mistake, weigh all your
evidence and facts carefully. Could be that your formal interview
will be enough and that nothing further will be required.

But if you do decide that something further has to be done,
remember that *the only purpose of punishment should be to correct*
—and nothing more. Don't be vindictive and revengeful about it.

By the same token, *say what you mean and mean what you say*.
Once I sat in on a group session where the boss was chewing us all
out for the poor quality of our work. He had us all ready and
anxious to really put out for him, but he blew it all with his last
sentence when he said, "Now I don't want any of you to worry; no
one's going to lose his job over this."

I've also found that a good method to use is to *let a man choose
his own punishment*. Ninety-nine out of a hundred will give themselves a more severe sentence than you would have. *Then you can
become his benefactor by reducing the punishment you didn't give
him*.

For that one out of a hundred who gives himself too light a sentence, tell him you're sorry, but that wasn't quite what you had in
mind. Then tell him what the punishment is going to be and stick
to your guns.

Ask for Cooperation

Ask for a person's cooperation and his help and you'll usually get it without question. Demand it or try to force a person to do things your way, and you'll get nowhere.

"Think you can handle it now, John?" or "See how to do it this way, Mary?" will get you much better cooperation than "Do it over, damn it, and you'd better get it right this time or else!"

Emphasize the Benefits to Be Gained

You'll get much further if you give the person an incentive for wanting to change his actions than if you were to merely issue him an order to do so.

For instance, Harry Kirkpatrick, district sales manager in St. Louis for Mutual of Omaha, tells me that the secret of keeping his salesmen motivated to work hard is not to preach to them about what the company wants, but to give them an incentive that will make them want to sell more insurance for their own benefit.

"I never tell them they have to do lots of legwork and call on lots of prospects if they want to work for me," Harry says. "Instead, I tell them that the more calls they make, the more insurance they'll sell, and the greater their income will be."

Finish with Sincere Praise and Appreciation

Don't end your interview on a sour note. Mix some honey with the vinegar. Criticism should leave a person with the idea he's been helped—not kicked.

So give him a pat on the back at the end of your session so you can finish with a friendly gesture. His last memory of your meeting should be a pat on the back, not a kick in the seat of the pants.

What to Do After the Interview

It's important that you follow up and make your criticism stick. Otherwise, all your efforts have been wasted. Here are five points you can use to make sure you get the results you're after.

1. Supervise to make sure corrective action is taken.
2. Praise the slightest improvement that is made.
3. Give your people a good reputation to live up to.
4. Follow up with another interview if necessary, but don't criticize too often.
5. Don't hold a grudge; forgive and forget.

18

How Miracle People Power
Can Make Others Want to
Do Their Best For You

When you use your miracle people power properly, people will want to do their best for you. They'll want to give it their all. You won't need to threaten, shout, browbeat, or coax them to get things done. Just use the techniques you'll find in this chapter, and you'll be able to get the maximum from them without having to settle for the bare minimum.

Remember that although all people have the same basic needs and desires, they still differ, one from another, primarily because *whatever a person is lacking at the moment he has the greatest need and desire for*. Therefore, if you want to get a person to do his best for you, you'll need to know what his most pressing requirement is so you can tailor your approach to fulfill that need.

When you use your miracle people power to bring out the best in people,

YOU'LL GAIN THESE BENEFITS

1. You won't have to accept just the bare minimum performance for them.
2. You'll be able to ask people to give their maximum effort for you.

3. If you're in business or industry, you'll realize increased sales or production.
4. You can look forward to lowered production costs and minimal business expenses.
5. When you get the best out of every person, it will mean increased profit, prestige, promotion, or perhaps all three for you.
6. No matter what you do, people will want to go all out for you.

TECHNIQUES YOU CAN USE TO GAIN THESE BENEFITS

Set the Example for People to Follow

If you want to get others to do their best for you, you should always set the example for them to follow. There are a lot of good character traits you ought to have, such as dependability, integrity, enthusiasm, loyalty, initiative, ingenuity, tact, unselfishness, judgment, and others.

To put these character traits to work for yourself so you can set the example, use these 11 guidelines:

1. Be at all times physically fit and mentally alert.
2. Always be the complete master of your emotions.
3. Maintain an optimistic and cheerful outlook and attitude.
4. Be enthusiastic about whatever you do.
5. Conduct yourself so that your personal habits will be above censure or reproach from anyone.
6. Cooperate in spirit as well as in fact.
7. Exercise initiative and ingenuity and encourage your people to do the same.
8. Be loyal to both your superiors and your subordinates.
9. Avoid the development of a clique of favorites.
10. Be tactful and courteous.
11. Be morally courageous. Stand for what you believe to be right.

Set High Standards for People to Attain

An excellent way to bring out a person's best is to set high standards for him to attain. I learned this from an army major, Charles T. McCampbell, when I was a young second lieutenant years and years ago.

I looked up to this man and admired him very much. He instilled in me the desire to do my best by showing me he had full confidence in me and in my abilities. He always expected me to give the maximum effort in whatever I did. "Do your best," he used to tell me. "You cannot do more; you should not want to do less."

One day he handed me an assignment with the terse comment, "Lieutenant, here's a tough job for you to do. I know you can handle it, or I wouldn't give it to you." Without saying another word, he turned sharply, and walked away.

When I first looked at the paper in my hand, I nearly panicked. At first glance, it seemed utterly impossible for me to accomplish. But at the same time, it never occurred to me not to try to do the job he'd given me to do. At least I had to try because he'd asked me to, and he'd shown complete confidence in my abilities to do so.

So I set to it and somehow managed to get the job done. After I'd completed it successfully, I realized that by setting such high standards and by showing complete confidence in me, he got far more out of me than I knew I was even capable of giving myself.

You can get the same results from your people, too, no matter what you do—whether you're an army officer, a preacher, teacher, businesswoman, salesman, foreman, supervisor, father, mother, etc.

You see, most people settle for far less than they're actually capable of doing. If you set a high standard for them, if you show them that you believe wholeheartedly they can do the job, they'll give you their absolute best. You'll get more out of them than they ever realized they had in them.

Always Give the Maximum Yourself

One of the best ways you can set the example for people to follow, and, at the same time, set high standards for them to attain, is to always give the maximum yourself. If you're not willing to give it

everything you've got, you don't have the right to expect other
people to give their best either. I've never known of any successful
company or business where the boss didn't work much longer and
harder than his employees.

A great many times giving your maximum simply means to
persevere, to hang in there, to not give up until the job is fully and
finally done. In fact, giving the maximum effort will often take a
persistence that President Calvin Coolidge once described this way:

> "Nothing in the world can take the place of persistence. Talent will
> not; nothing is more common than unsuccessful men with talent.
> Genius will not; the world is full of educated derelicts. Persistence and
> determination alone are omnipotent. The slogan 'Press on!' has solved
> and always will solve the problem of the human race."

How to Give a Person's Job Meaning and Purpose

Good employees do not enjoy doing their jobs on a day-to-day
basis with no other purpose in mind than their weekly paychecks.
They will do much better work for you if they know your long-range
plans and if they understand the relationship between their daily
work and the larger company goals and objectives. Your people
are entitled to know not only *what* they are expected to do, but also
why they're doing it, and *where* it's going to lead them.

For instance, don't ask merely that the operating costs of a
department be gone over to find out where reductions can be made
and simply let it go at that. You'll get far better results if you
explain that this cost analysis is part of a long-range plan to provide
the extra profit margin that will be needed for future salary increases.

Then the people who are going to compile that information for
you will be able to see a direct benefit for themselves in doing this
detailed and tedious work. Besides that, they'll realize that by cutting
costs, they will be contributing their share to strengthening the
operating efficiency of the company, and thus helping to insure their
own job security.

Of course, I realize that it takes some extra time and effort on
your part to explain the why, the how, and the wherefore of a job
to a person. In fact, you might well wonder if it's really all worth it.
I can assure you that it is, and here's why:

A labor union and the management of a company made a joint study of three thousand of its employees to find out what they wanted most from their jobs, and how they rated those wants in their order of importance. The results showed that the employees wanted, first of all, to receive credit for the work they did. Second, they wanted to have an interesting job to do. Fair pay with salary increases came in third.

The results of this study greatly surprised both the labor union and the management of the company. They had both expected fair pay and salary increases to be in first place rather than down in third.

I think you can easily see from this how important it is to give meaning and purpose to your people's jobs, if you want to get the best from them. Your extra effort to do so can make the difference between getting the bare minimum or the maximum performance from each individual.

How to Get a Person Emotionally Involved

You'll never get the best out of a person unless you appeal to his heart as well as his head, for as I've told you before, *the head never hears 'til the heart has listened.*

You see, you can give a person all sorts of logical reasons why he ought to do a job a certain way, but you're only appealing to his intellect. You must make your pitch to his emotional instincts to really get him involved. The more motives you can appeal to, the greater your opportunities for success.

How do you appeal to a person's emotions? Easy. You simply show him the benefits he's going to gain when he succeeds in reaching his goal. It's been proven time and again that when a person really wants to succeed at what he's doing, he can do superlative work where before he failed.

Just for instance, a D or F student can turn around and make the dean's list when he is properly motivated and when he has a fixed goal and purpose in mind. A dissident malcontent can also become your most dependable worker when he's really inspired.

To make this technique work, to get a person to do his best for you, you should give him a specific goal to shoot for, you should make it possible for him to reach that goal, and you should also make the reward worthwhile when he does achieve it.

1. How to Give Him a Specific Goal to Shoot for. You will be surprised at how quickly a definite goal in black and white can change a person's attitude from vague generalities to exact and meaningful specifics.

Perhaps one person's goal will be to make more money on the job. Then show him what he has to do to reach that goal. Maybe another man is interested in getting a new and different job. Tell him what he must learn and be capable of doing before he can be considered for it.

If you help a person establish his own goals and then give him every bit of help you can to reach them, you won't have to push him any longer to get him to do his best for you. He'll become his own self-starter.

2. How to Give Him a Goal He Can Reach. Don't give a person a goal that's too difficult or too distant for him to reach. Take a student starting out on the long slow grind to become a doctor of medicine, for instance. He'll have to give himself some intermediate goals so he can pace himself for the long haul, or he might not be able to make it. First, he'll need to make his goal his bachelor's degree; then on to medical school; after that, his internship; finally, his own private practice as a physician or surgeon.

No matter what the person's goal is, cutting it up into intermediate steps will make it more attainable for him. For instance, my daughter wanted to be able to type without errors at a speed of 75 words a minute.

"Teresa, give yourself a goal of 50, then 55, 60, and so on," I told her. "If you don't, you'll get too discouraged and quit long before you reach your final goal."

3. How to Make the Reward Exciting and Worthwhile. A person will never be able to reach his final goal unless the reward is exciting and worthwhile. Attainment of his goal must give him a reward that will fulfill one or more of his basic needs and desires. For example, you say to a woman, "Sue, if you'll do a better job for me, I'll recommend you for promotion."

Now this statement by itself is not enough to get Sue to do her best for you. She cannot see the reward clearly enough. She must be able to visualize how she can gain certain benefits from that promotion. She'll need to know if the reward she gains is worth all the effort she's going to expend.

So it's up to you to tell her how she'll be able to earn more money . . . how she'll have increased importance, prestige, and status . . . how her co-workers will respect her even more. That way you make the reward exciting and worthwhile, so she'll do her best to reach the goal you've set for her.

How to Get His Eyes off the Ground

No matter what a person does, you can get him to do it better if he'll just get his eyes off the ground. Let me give you one of the best examples I've ever seen of making the most of a so-called menial job.

Fred Wilson was once a night janitor at the Kraft Foods plant in Springfield, Missouri, when I worked there many years ago on the graveyard shift as a supervisor. All he could see ahead for himself was a long row of sleepless nights, year after year. "All I know how to do is sweep and scrub floors," he told me one night.

"Then why don't you take what you know and go into the janitorial business for yourself, Fred," I said. "There are a lot of big department stores and other businesses in town that would gladly pay for a dependable regular cleaning service."

Today Fred has the custodial contracts for many of the big stores and factories in Springfield. He also has a residential division in his company that provides a regular monthly maintenance service for homes and apartment buildings. Fred transformed a thankless job into a profitable business simply by looking up at the stars instead of down at the dirt on his feet.

How to Emphasize Skill and Results—Not Rules

You should be interested in results—not methods. As long as the accomplishment of the mission doesn't infringe upon the welfare of your people, you should not care how the job is done—just as long as it is done, and done well.

You've already seen back in Chapter 13 how the employees of Gaines, Monsanto Chemical, Motorola, Skyline, and many others did far better work and made less mistakes when they were given full responsibility and authority for doing their jobs.

It's a proven fact that when you emphasize skill and results rather than rules, when you give a person the responsibility and the authority to do the job, he can be up to 10 times as effective as others in getting his work done. Here are eight proven methods you can use to emphasize skill and results—not rules:

1. Have Complete Confidence in the Person. Let him know that you expect him to do his best. Nearly everyone tends to perform as closely as possible to what is expected of him. When your people know that you expect them to do a superior job, and that you have every confidence in their ability to deliver, that's what they'll usually give you.

2. Don't Dominate a Person or Over-Supervise Him. Your subordinates will like to know that you are available for advice and counsel when they need you. However, they will resent over-supervision and harassment. Individual initiative is best developed when they can use their imagination in developing their own methods and techniques to do their jobs.

3. Throw Down a Challenge. A challenge will bring out the best, even in the most average person. Nothing motivates a good man more than to find out that he is better than he thought, or to prove to others that he can do a better job than they thought he could. This method will also help discover your best people for you so they can be pinpointed for future more important responsibilities.

4. Besides Financial Security, Offer a Person Psychic Security in the form of approval, recognition of efforts, self-respect, and self-reliance. When a person succeeds in completing a difficult task, he will have achieved much more than just monetary reward. He'll gain recognition from others for a job well done, and he'll have increased confidence in himself and in his own abilities. Remember the study made by the labor union and management of the company and use its findings to your own advantage.

5. Encourage Him to Set Some Personal Goals of His Own. I've already shown you how to make a person want to do his best for you by setting certain goals for him to attain. But he, too, must be able to visualize his own personal goals. These personal goals are extremely important, for if he can achieve them, then the attainment of your goals will be much easier to realize.

6. Let a Man Be Himself. Unless long hair and beards are safety factors in a man's work, they should have no bearing on a man's job security or his promotion status. My father-in-law used to say, "You can't trust a man with a mustache," so of course I immediately grew one.

If you can, have a flexible work schedule for your people. For instance, employees at the Hewlett-Packard plant in Palo Alto, California, come to work any time between 6.30 and 8.30 A.M. They leave when they've completed an eight hour work day. This system has proven to be extremely satisfactory for everyone.

7. Let the Person Tell You How and Where He Needs to Improve. No matter how good you are in your ability to criticize another person, remember that self-criticism is still a much better motivator. To get a man to evaluate himself, call him in once in a while and tell him about his good points. Then ask him to tell you about his weak points and how he plans to correct them. Use criticism yourself only as a last resort.

8. Use Praise and Encouragement. You reward a person when you praise and encourage him and when you show him how much you appreciate his efforts for you. Everyone thrives on appreciation. Praising in public is especially beneficial, for public praise increases a person's prestige and status, it raises his morale and strengthens his self-confidence. Public recognition of a man's efforts is one of the best ways to gain his help, his loyalty, and his support.

19

How to Use Your Miracle
People Power to Handle
Problem People

Problem people require special methods and take extra attention because they are potential or actual troublemakers. They can wreck good friendly relationships and create havoc in any group.

Every factory or store, department or section, group or organization of any kind always has a certain percentage of problem people. If they are allowed to go their own willful way unchecked, they can cause a great deal of harm or damage to you.

What Is a Problem Person?

It's important, first of all, that you know how to determine whether a person actually is or is not a problem to you. A lot of people will disagree on this point. Some will say a problem person is a nonconformist, an offbeat individual who speaks, thinks or acts differently than the norm. Others will say he's a neurotic or a maladjusted person. Most people tend to classify an individual with long hair or a beard as a problem personality. Members of any unorthodox religious movement are regarded by many as out-of-step or freaky.

But as a matter of fact, a person might be any one of these, and still not be a problem at all to anyone.

No matter what other people say, you need answer only one question to determine whether a person is a problem to you or not. *Is this person causing you damage or harm in some way?* If he is, he's a problem to you and you need do something to correct this situation. If he's not causing you harm or damage, *regardless of his appearance, dress, or behavior,* then you don't have a problem person on your hands after all, and you need do absolutely nothing about him. Don't let personal dislikes or prejudices mislead you.

Once you grasp and understand this simple concept of what a problem person really is, you're actually much better informed in this business of handling problem people than a lot of the personnel managers who make this their full-time job.

To sum up this idea, then, *a problem person must cause you harm or damage in some way,* or he is not a problem person to you at all.

What's the Percentage of Problem People in Any Group?

Statistically speaking, 100 people can be classified this way:

Group A: Five persons will be self-motivating.

Group B: Ten must be challenged to develop their full potential.

Group C: Seventy must be stimulated by competent leadership to do their best.

Group D: *Ten are difficult to handle, present constant problems to you, and require extra effort.*

Group E: Five are completely incorrigible.

Out of every 100 persons, the miracle people power techniques you've learned in the previous chapters will handle easily the 85 listed in Groups A, B, and C. The five found in Group E are completely incorrigible, and can usually be found in jails, reformatories, and penitentiaries. They are beyond the scope of this book since I have not covered the field of abnormal psychology.

This chapter, then, will be devoted to the people in Group D—the

10 out of every 100 who are difficult to handle, give you problems, and will require extra effort on your part to get the job done.

Paul Newport's Experience

Is it worth all that extra effort to handle a problem person? I think so, and so does Paul Newport, the director of personnel management for the Illinois Power and Light Company. "Every time I'm inclined to give up on a person and say to hell with it all, I remember a fellow named Scott Brady," Mr. Newport says.

"I was in the army then, a training company commander at Fort Carson, Colorado. Scott Brady was transferred to my unit. He'd been in the army 21 weeks and still hadn't finished his first 8 weeks of basic training. He'd been AWOL or in the stockade most of that time.

"When he came to my company, I made our status extremely clear to him. 'I don't care what you've done before,' I said. 'All that matters is what you do for me now. If you'll soldier for me, I'll back you all the way. Your past will be wiped clean. It's all up to you.'

"Scott ended up as the company's honor graduate. He wasn't really bad at all. He'd just gotten off on the wrong foot, and everybody expected the worst from him, so they treated him that way. I started him off with a clean slate. I held no prejudice whatever against him for his past mistakes. All that counted as far as I was concerned was what he did for me. I gave him the chance to succeed and he did.

"So every time I'm tempted to give up on someone here, I remember Scott Brady, and I try to give the person another chance. I know I can't win 'em all, but I'm going to get as many as I can."

Sometimes the opportunity to prove himself is all the problem person needs. At other times, it will take something more. That's why I've included other techniques you can use to reach the difficult individual. When you use them,

YOU'LL GAIN THESE BENEFITS

Of course, if the difficult person is a problem person who works for you, you'll want to do something positive to protect your investment of time, money, and training in him. If you don't, you'll end up like the army does, replacing a man every 2 or 3 years. Few companies can really afford a personnel turnover like that, for they can't train skilled replacements at the taxpayer's expense as the armed services do.

Or suppose the person doesn't work for you. Using your miracle people power to influence a difficult boss can pay you dividends in the form of a raise, promotion, increased authority, and prestige. Or it can mean establishing harmonious relationships with a recalcitrant and sullen co-worker. You can also use your miracle people power to turn a competitor into a friend instead of an enemy. You can even transform the grouchy next-door neighbor into a friendly helpful human being by making an extra effort with him.

You'll have a tremendous sense of self-accomplishment, for learning how to handle difficult or problem people is like a kind of postgraduate course in human relations. You'll master new and exciting techniques to cope with the problem person.

And as you do, you'll broaden beyond measure your miracle people power to manage people in general. As you learn how to change a destructive, recalcitrant, don't-give-a-damn person into a helpful, worthwhile individual, your miracle power to handle all people will go far beyond your most optimistic expectations. In all truth, you will really be amazed at your ability to get things done through people—things you never thought possible to do before.

TECHNIQUES YOU CAN USE TO GAIN THESE BENEFITS

How to Find the *Real* Reason Behind What a Person Says or Does

It's important that you find the real reason behind what a person says or does so you can help him solve his problem. You can best do this by skillfully asking questions and carefully listening to the answers. You'll need to learn how to listen between the lines, too, for many times what a person does *not* say will tell you much more than what he does say.

"A negative emotion is usually the primary reason for problems between two people," says Dr. Howard Pickering, a Milwaukee,

Wisconsin, psychiatrist. "For instance, marital difficulties can arise from the husband or wife being overly jealous. A person who is emotionally insecure will usually be extremely selfish, suspicious, and grasping. It's important to ascertain what experience in the past caused this person to develop such a negative attitude before you can help him solve his problem."

How Lonnie Robertson Handled Harry

You don't have to be a psychiatrist like Doctor Pickering to find out why a person has a negative attitude. You could be a department foreman like Lonnie Robertson.

Lonnie had a worker named Harry who was a constant complainer. Nothing was ever correct. The company was wrong . . . the foreman was never right . . . his co-workers were all bums . . . the whole world was no good, according to Harry. He despised any kind of authority. It made him fighting mad to have a foreman or supervisor watch him or check his work.

Lonnie was determined to find out what was wrong with Harry. Weeks of one-sided conversation went by. Slowly he pieced together Harry's background. He checked Harry's personnel records and found he'd been a POW for more than a year during the Korean War.

Lonnie began to probe deeper and deeper into this aspect of Harry's past. He came to realize that the primary reason Harry detested authority so much was because his Korean captors had treated him so badly and he'd been unable to do anything whatever about it. Harry was taking out his past frustrations and spite on the people with authority in his present.

After Harry found someone he could trust to talk to about his horrible experience, he began to change his negative attitude rapidly. He was able to unload and rid himself of his bitterness about the past. After this emotional catharsis, he found himself free and able to face life with an optimistic attitude and a positive approach.

Fear Can Cause a Negative Emotion, Too

Many times a person's negative attitude will arise because he hasn't been able to fulfill one of his innermost needs and desires. His fear that he will not be able to do so comes to the surface to influence all his transactions with other people for fear is the reverse side of the coin of desire.

Back in Chapter 3, I listed the eleven basic fears that many people have at one time or another in life. I mentioned there that a primary motivator for most people with a negative attitude or a sour outlook on life is self-centered fear: the fear that they might lose something they already possess, or the fear they will fail to gain something they are trying to attain.

When you discover what a person's fear is, a great many times you'll also find the *real* reason behind what he says or does. Then you can use your miracle people power to help him get rid of his fear and solve his problem.

How to Identify the Problem Person Who Works for You

When you know what to look for, it's easy for you to identify the problem person who works for you. To cause you harm or damage, he must be hurting your production, your sales, or your profit. All you need do is ask yourself these three simple concise questions about him. If you can't honestly answer *yes* to at least one of them, he's not your problem; you'll have to look elsewhere.

1. **Is His Job Performance Below Standard?** Is the person's work below the accepted norm in both quality and quantity? Does he produce fewer units than he should in an average work day? Does he always have less sales than anyone else at the end of every week? In short, *does the person in some specific way fail to measure up to reasonable performance standards you've set for him?* If he does, he's costing you money and you have a problem person on your hands.

2. **Does He Interfere with the Performance of Others?** Is this person a constant source of irritation, annoyance, or interference? Do you usually find him at the bottom of employee disturbances? Does he keep other people from doing their best work? Does the quality or the quantity of his work slow down or keep another section or group from functioning properly? Does he cause some of his co-workers to lose incentive pay because of his carelessness? If so —this person definitely is a problem to you.

   3. **Does He Cause Harm to the Co-Workers in His Group?** The
reputation or good name of any group can be damaged even if only
one of its members is a chronic troublemaker. He can keep the rest
of his group constantly on edge by his actions. For instance, if one
member of a professional athletic team gets out of line, he gives the
entire team a problem. One troublesome sales representative can
give the entire company a bad name. If any of your people have
ever caused you to get a complaint, have an order cancelled, or lose
a customer by his carelessness and indifference—you have a problem
to take care of.

How to Handle the Problem Person Who Works for You

   Once you've identified the problem person, what are you going to
do about him? Well, it's either get rid of him or change him. If you
can't fire him or if you don't want to do that, then you'll have to do
something else. So ask yourself just what can be changed.
   Would you be able to change the person's behavior? Can you
change his attitude in some way? Can you change the situation?
What can you do to improve this problem person who works for
you? Let's look at some specific examples and see what others
would do.

   PROBLEM: Ted L. is an alcoholic. He comes in late, does poor
   work, calls in sick several days a week. However, when he's sober, he
   turns out better quality workmanship than anyone else. Has been with
   the company 18 years.
   SOLUTION: Get in touch with a member of Alcoholics Anonymous. Have him contact Ted and talk to him. Chances are there's a
   recovered alcoholic working for you right now and you don't even
   know it. Tell Ted what you're going to do and let him know it's either
   AA or his job. The point is you've offered him a solution, but you
   can go no farther than that. Don't try to carry the man; just show him
   how to carry his load.

   PROBLEM: Pete K. is not doing his job properly. Quality control
   turns back 75 percent of his production. Yet Pete is serious and sincere about his work and seems to be trying hard to do a good job.
   SOLUTION: If Pete doesn't have the basic skills to do his job, then
   he should receive further training and instruction until he is properly

qualified. If this doesn't work, then it could be the job is beyond his capabilities. If so, he should be given less demanding duties to perform.

PROBLEM: John D. seems to spend more time in the lounge drinking coffee than he does at his desk. Constantly bothering other people with idle chatter and conversation.

SOLUTION: Give him more work to do. A person who doesn't have enough to do to keep busy is a potent source of trouble. Not only will he become bored and apathetic, but at the same time, his co-workers will also be extremely envious of him. Through the years, I've seen examples time after time where one person has too little to do while another person is overloaded. Be sure *all* your people have enough work to keep them busy. Consolidate or eliminate some jobs if necessary.

PROBLEM: George C. is a constant source of irritation to his supervisor. There seems to be a definite personality clash between them.

SOLUTION: Sometimes people do clash without any logical or visible reason. If the friction between George and his supervisor can't be ironed out peacefully, then transfer George to a different job. I must admit that I, too, have met a few people in my time I wouldn't care to work either with or for. Nor would I want them as next-door neighbors either.

PROBLEM: Entire department turning out slipshod, careless, and shoddy workmanship. Evidence of a lackadaisical and indifferent attitude on everyone's part.

SOLUTION: Better supervision is necessary. Poor supervision can turn even the best employee into a problem person. You can't expect people to give their utmost for you if you never check on them. A person is always as lazy as he dares to be. *Never inspected—always neglected* is a good motto to keep in mind.

How to Handle Other Problem People

It could be that some of the specific problem people in your life are your boss, the person who works beside you, a business competitor, or a grouchy neighbor. Just ask yourself the test question (Is this person causing me damage or harm in some way?) before you decide whether the other individual is a problem person or not.

For instance, let's just suppose it's a grouchy neighbor who's

giving you fits. Don't try to get even with him. That will only make
things worse. Instead, find out what's wrong if you can and try to
help the person solve his problem. If you can't find out what's
bothering him, give of yourself and help him anyway. Let me give
you a practical example of that point.

Once there were two neighbors, Jim and George, who could not
get along with each other. Jim and his wife had three growing
children; George and Eloise were childless and they demanded
absolute peace and quiet, even throughout the daytime, a literal
impossibility in the summertime when there are three healthy active
children around.

There were other problems as well, most of them, though, having
to do with noise. Jim's wife even gave up playing the piano for if
the windows were open, the moment she did, the phone would ring.
Or if Jim made a little too much noise in his garage workshop on
Saturday or Sunday afternoon, the same thing would happen.

Jim was deeply hurt and disturbed, for he'd never run into a situation like this before. He simply didn't know how to handle it. Time
and again he tried to establish a friendly and cordial relationship
with George, but he couldn't break through his hard shell of enmity
so he finally gave up. Even when their lawnmowers nearly rubbed
wheels along their backyard battle lines, they never spoke to each
other.

Then one summer George and Eloise went on vacation. At first
Jim didn't even realize they were gone. But one evening after he'd
mowed his yard, he saw how high George's grass was. It was an open
invitation to a burgler for it was a sure sign no one was home.

"A sudden thought came to me," Jim says. *"Don't try to love your
neighbor . . . just help him*. I looked at that high grass again and my
mind rebelled. Help George? Rubbish. After the way he's treated
me and my wife? No dice; nothing doing."

But the next morning the same thought persisted in Jim's mind. It
refused to go away, so he finally gave up and mowed George's lawn.

A day later, George and Eloise came back. Within an hour
George was knocking at Jim's door. When Jim opened it, George
said belligerently, "Did you mow my yard? I've asked everyone in
the whole neighborhood. Jack says you did. I don't believe it. Did
you?"

"Yes, George, I did," Jim said. "Why, is something wrong?"

"No, nothing's wrong," George said. He turned and walked away. Then he stopped, turned, and with a great deal of effort said, "Thanks."

So the ice was broken for Jim and George. Months of bitter silence was gone. Oh, they're not playing golf or bridge together, and their wives don't have coffee together in the morning nor do they borrow salt and sugar yet. But progress is being made.

Love your neighbor? Could be, but as far as I'm concerned, it works only if you spell *love* H-E-L-P. How can I be so sure of that? That's easy. *I'm Jim.*

There is not enough time or space to cover every problem situation with each person such as your boss, your co-worker, your competitor, and so on, but this principle can be used most of the time with all of them. Just remember, don't try to love a person—just *help* him solve his problem. Out of that small beginning will grow friendship and mutual understanding.

20

How Miracle People Power Can Fill Your Home Life with Excitement, Joy, and Real Happiness

Some people work overtime to get along with everyone outside the home—their friends, neighbors, co-workers, business associates, church members, and so on—but do absolutely nothing at all to create a happy and joyous atmosphere in their own home.

"People who treat their family worse than they do their friends figure they have a captive audience who can do nothing about the situation," says Doctor Curtis Springer, a clinical psychologist who specializes in marital counseling. "They fail to realize how really happy their lives could be if they would only use as much courtesy, diplomacy, and tact with their own families as they do with others in their daily activities."

Do you have this problem in your own home? Do you take out your frustrations from your business or your work on your family? If you do, then this step will be helpful to you. Or if your family life just seems to lack something, if you feel it isn't what it could or should be, then you can use this step, too. In it you will learn how you can use your miracle people power to gain such benefits as excitement, joy, and real happiness in your home life.

TECHNIQUES YOU CAN USE TO GAIN THESE 3 BENEFITS

How to Choose the Kind of Home Life You Want

Each and every one of us possesses a power that we often fail to use properly. *That power is the freedom of choice.* Many people choose poverty when they need only to choose riches. Some choose failure instead of success. Others choose to be afraid of life when all they need do is step out with courage and take what is rightfully theirs.

What you do about your family life is the same. You have the power to choose the kind of home life you want. You can choose one that is fun: one that is filled with excitement, joy, and happiness. Or you can choose a home life that is constantly filled with resentments, anger, arguments, and bickering. It's all up to you.

I once had an uncle whom I admired greatly, William Roland. Uncle Bill and Aunt Margaret were married for more than 60 years when he died. They seemed always to be wonderfully happy with each other. I never once heard a cross word from either of them for the other, nor did I ever see an angry glance exchanged between them.

Just before I was married, Uncle Bill asked me to come by his house to chat with him. "Will you accept a small bit of advice from your uncle?" he asked. When I said that I would be glad to, here's what he told me.

"You can be happy in your marriage if you just choose to be," he said. "That's what your Aunt Margaret and I did when we were married many years ago. We chose to be happy. If you want your marriage to be a good one, you should do the same.

"Sure, there'll be ups and downs. You won't be living on the mountain top every day . . . no one can do that. You'll have some valleys in between that will be filled with sorrow and heartaches and sadness. Your Aunt Margaret and I have had those bad days, too, but we've weathered all those storms because we made up our minds at the very start to be happy in our marriage no matter what happened.

"So if you choose to be happy in your marriage right here and now at the very beginning, and your wife, Belva, does the same, then no matter what happens, your marriage will be a successful one."

The worth of that advice has not been dimmed by the years. As far as I'm concerned, it's still good so I'm passing it along to you. I've found it to be most valuable in my more than 30 years of marriage.

Even if you've been married a long time, it's still not too late to make the choice to be happy with your wife or your husband. No matter how bad things might seem to be at times, they'll always get better when you make that simple decision.

How to Keep Your Marriage Fresh and Alive

One of the quickest ways I know of for a marriage to go sour and lose its zing and sparkle is to take your partner for granted. A lot of married couples don't realize it takes as much effort to keep a spouse as it did to get one in the first place.

Just for example, a woman goes all out to get her man. She primps, powders, perfumes, dresses up, looks like a doll, and really butters him up. Then she marries him, sits down, and lets herself go completely to pot. In a few short years, she gains 30 to 40 pounds, gets slovenly and sloppy, and could care less. After all, she's captured her prey; she has her husband. As far as she is concerned, the hunt is over. And then she wonders why her husband becomes unfaithful and ends up with a mistress.

If, as a woman, you're guilty of taking your husband for granted like that, here's what you can do to get yourself out of that rut right now before it's too late.

Forget your own needs and desires completely. Be more concerned with what he wants than with what you want. And what is one of the things he wants most of all? A sexually attractive woman who looks just about like the girl he fell in love with and married. So start right now to take off those extra pounds. Stop going to bed with curlers in your hair and cold cream smeared all over your face. Instead, bathe and make yourself more desirable with perfumes and powders and all those sexy smelly feminine things.

In the morning, make yourself attractive at breakfast time. Start the day off with a fresh dress and a cheerful smile. Throw away that old sloppy bathrobe and those bedroom slippers that are so big they flop and flap with every step you take. When he comes home at night from work, wear a clean bright dress. Greet him with a kiss and a hug, no matter how tired and worn-out you are.

Keep yourself attractive for your man at all times—morning, noon, and night—and he'll always be your husband, not someone else's boyfriend.

Now men are just as guilty as women about taking their partners for granted. A man works his head off to catch the girl he loves. He plays the part of the perfect gentleman until the minister says, "I now pronounce you man and wife." Then he figures his courting days are finished so he assumes the attitude of the Ozark Mountain man who says, "The best way to keep your wife is to keep her pregnant, barefooted, and in the kitchen." From then on he takes his wife completely for granted. She's just another piece of furniture to him; that is, until she files for divorce charging him with cruelty and neglect.

You may not have let things go this far, but if you are guilty of taking your wife for granted, if your home life is not as happy as it ought to be, here's what you can do to change that situation.

You need to pay more attention to what your wife wants than what you want. If you forget yourself and help her fulfill her basic needs and desires, you'll always keep your marriage fresh and alive. For instance, one of the best ways to do that is to give her your honest thanks and appreciation for what she is to you and what she does for you. That's the next technique I want to take up right now.

How to Give Thanks and Honest Appreciation to Your Wife

Now it's a smart thing to surprise your wife with an occasional gift on times other than birthdays, wedding anniversaries, and Christmas. But you don't have to send her flowers or candy every other day just to show her how much you appreciate her. My method costs you absolutely nothing and it's even more effective.

I know a couple who've been happily married for more than 35 years now, and I happen to know for a fact this man never gives his wife any presents except on those standard occasions of her birthday, their wedding anniversary, and Christmas.

"What's your secret of marital happiness, Morgan?" I asked him.

"Very simple, Jim," he said. "I give my whole-hearted attention to my wife. I always let her know by what I say and do that I appreciate her. I still say *please* and *thank you,* even after all these years. And I never get up from the table without saying, 'Thanks, dear; that was a wonderful meal,' or 'Thanks a million, honey; you sure are a terrific cook.'

"Or when we pass each other in the house, I always reach out and brush her hand gently or pat her on the—well, you know. Always keeps a woman feeling young and desirable no matter how old she is when you pat her that way.

"Or I take her a cup of tea in the afternoon when she's knitting or sewing or watching television. What if she doesn't want it? What if she's not thirsty? Don't worry about that. She'll drink it anyway just because I've shown my appreciation for her. And I always place a glass of ice water on her night stand when we go to bed. Maybe she pours it down the sink during the night for all I know, but it's always empty in the morning."

I suppose these points might seem tiny and inconsequential to you at first. They might not sound like much at all, but just as Morgan says, they serve as proof positive to your wife that you still love her and that you still appreciate her. Never kid yourself. It's the tiny, inconsequential things that make or break a marriage much more than the big ones.

So if you want to have a harmonious relationship and a pleasant atmosphere in your home, if you want to use your miracle people power to fill your home life with excitement, joy, and real happiness, then give thanks and honest appreciation to your wife all the time.

When you do, you'll be mighty happy, I can assure you of that. For when you do these little things for her, your benefits will multiply, too. I'll guarantee you'll never want for a clean shirt, you'll never put on a pair of unpressed pants, nor will you ever sit down to a cold supper. Your wife will love all those *little inconsequential extras* and she'll want to make sure you keep them coming.

Here's One of the Real Secrets
to Joy and Happiness in Your Home

One of the real secrets to complete joy and happiness in your home is *accepting your partner as he or she is*. In other words, don't try to change your partner and make him or her over. Don't nag or criticize. You'll never change a person that way.

Take your own husband for instance. Have you ever been able to change him very much through all your years of marriage? I know you probably started out to remake him into the person you thought he ought to be, but did you ever really succeed? I doubt it; I know my own wife never did.

Or if you're thinking of remaking your wife over to fit your own specifications, forget it. I failed at that one, too. I haven't been able to change her one bit through all these years. She's still the same as when I married her. But now I'm happy that I failed. I realize I couldn't have improved on her at all.

This is a most valuable point for you to remember. *The only person you can ever really change or control in your life is you, yourself, and you alone—no one else*. So accept your partner just as he or she is. You'll be much happier when you do.

Just for instance, I once knew a woman who had a real problem with her husband and wanted to change him. Mrs. J. had a family of four children and a husband who'd been drunk and out of work for most of their 20 years of marriage. She had supported the family the majority of that time herself by working in a department store.

Every possible treatment and approach that had been used to solve his drinking problem had failed. None had given him any lasting relief. For specific religious reasons, Mrs. J. did not want to divorce her husband, but she could not accept him the way he was. And since she could not change him, her unhappiness and her children's unhappiness grew deeper and deeper.

Then one day she made an important discovery. "There is absolutely nothing I can do to change John or to solve his drinking problem," she told herself. "But that is his problem—not mine. I'm as powerless to change him or to solve his problem as he is—in fact, even more so. I cannot live his life for him. He is a sick man and I am going to give up the idea that he ever can or ever will stop drinking. From now on I am not going to torture myself with him or his problem any more. I am going to accept things just the way they are.

"I will take care of him, of course, for he is still my husband, and I love him in spite of everything. But I am going to quit trying to change him. I am going to accept him as he is and do what I can to make my own life and the lives of my children as happy as possible under these circumstances."

Mrs. J. was admitting to herself that she was powerless to change her husband. Her new concept of the situation worked wonders both for herself and her children. It did not stop her husband from drinking; it could not do that. But in spite of his drinking, they all began to live comparatively normal lives again.

Realizing that you cannot possibly change your wife or husband can help you the same way. In fact, you'll never be able to achieve total joy and happiness in your marriage until you do accept them exactly as they are.

How to Be an Exceptional Sexual Partner

A marriage cannot possibly be unified, loving, and mutually satisfactory if the act of sexual intercourse is not also unified, loving, and mutually satisfactory.

Now this is not a book on how to solve physical sexual problems. I don't pretend to be an expert in that field. There are any number of good marriage manuals on the market that can help you if harmonious physical sex relations with your mate is a problem in your life.

However, I do know that a negative mental attitude has as much to do, if not more, with sexual incompatibility as physical ineptitude. So I'd like to give you two small points that will help turn you from a selfish sexual partner who's interested only in himself or herself and his or her self-satisfaction into one whose primary aim is to fulfill the needs and desires of the mate.

1. Make love *with*—not *to*—your partner.
2. After every act of sexual intercourse, show your appreciation to your mate. Say "Thank you."

Two small points, I know, and at first glance, you might think they are hardly worth your while. All I ask you to do is use them for a short time. You'll find they can change you into an exceptional sexual partner who treats the other person with tender loving care instead of as a physical love object.

How to Work and Play Together

If you're a man, it's important that you spend part of your free time with your wife doing the things she likes to do. Don't let her become a golf widow as so many men do. That's no way to keep a marriage intact. If she's athletically inclined, take her along with you when you go bowling, swimming, or boating. If that's not her thing, if she'd rather see a movie or go dancing, then do what she wants to do, at least part of the time.

By the same token, if you're the wife, don't usurp all your husband's free time for your preferred activities. If he likes to play some poker one night a week or get together once in a while to drink beer and shoot the breeze with some of his buddies, don't be jealous. You're entitled to some time of your own to do the things only women like to do, too, so do the same favor for him. Just be reasonable with your demands on each other's time.

The same thing holds true when it comes to working around the house. Do it together. Most men think it's degrading for some reason to help their wives with the dishes. Yet those same men like to play head chef at the backyard barbecue.

You might not like to do "woman's work" like cooking, washing dishes, or scrubbing floors every day of the week, but your wife will sure appreciate the help at least once in a while.

At least, don't be like Ed K., a fellow who used to live next door to me. Ed would come home, plop in his easy chair, and yell for Arline to bring him the evening paper, his slippers, and a beer.

He never lifted a finger to help his wife after supper or any other time either, for that matter. He refused to take care of his two small sons while she did the dishes. His attitude was that he'd worked hard at the office all day and he had a right to relax. He simply didn't want his family to bother him in *his* free time.

If you treat your wife like this, it's a good way to end up living all alone. That's exactly what happened to Ed.

How to Enjoy Your Children

As you can tell from the heading above, this small section is not going to teach you how to raise your children. I'm going to use it only to give you one little tip that will show you *how to enjoy your children* even more than you do right now. I learned this secret from a friend of mine, Ray Turner.

"One summer a few years ago when Gary was 16, he and I went on a month long trip throughout the west in a camper, just the 2 of us. We did everything together just as 2 buddies would. We took turns driving the pickup truck, cooking the meals, washing the dishes, and making the beds. Not once during that month did I assume a father-son relationship with him. I treated him as an equal.

"When we were back home, Gary paid me a compliment I'll always remember. 'Dad, this has been the best trip of my life,' he said. 'I'll always remember it, for you've shown me that you can be my friend as well as my father.' "

I know you have to give guidance and counsel to your children, but if you really want to enjoy them completely, drop that parent role as often as you can and be their friend as well as their father or mother. It will bring you a wonderful new relationship with them.

21

How to Keep Your Miracle People Power at a High Level All Your Life

For 20 chapters, I've given you techniques you can use to gain miracle people power. I know I've covered a vast area, so I'd like to use this final chapter as sort of a small summary or wrap-up of what has gone before.

Now you might wonder if the benefits to be gained are worth the efforts to be expended. As far as I'm concerned, the benefit of achieving miracle people power is well worth all the work involved, but you'll have to answer that question for yourself. One of the best ways to do this is look around you at some of the people you know or with whom you work. I'm sure you'll find someone who is practicing most of the techniques I've given you in this book.

What kind of person will that individual be? Well, I think you will find that he's happy, serene, and contented with life. He will be well adjusted and able to get along with almost everyone without friction.

I knew a man very much like that once. Let me tell you about him. Perhaps you'll know someone just about like him or at least you'll know someone who has many of the same character attributes this gentleman had. I've already mentioned his name to you before back in Chapter 18. He was Charles T. McCampbell.

Charles T. McCampbell was a United States Army Major I met way back in World War II. Major McCampbell knew his job as an army officer and he knew it well. He conducted himself as a gentleman at all times. I never once saw him lose his temper. This is not to say that he never felt anger, but that he always kept his emotions under tight control, no matter how trying the circumstances.

Although he was intensely loyal to his superiors, he had no fear of them. He also stuck up for his own people and was just as loyal to them, too. He was frank and honest, and said what he meant and meant what he said. In all the years I knew him he never lied, nor did he ever once fail to keep his word. He never abused his privileges as an officer, as some were often prone to do.

The Major had a sense of humor and didn't make the mistake of taking himself too seriously. He was kind, decent, courteous, and he fully respected the rights of others. Although he felt responsible for setting the example for his subordinates to follow, he didn't place himself on a pedestal, nor did he become a sanctimonious bore by preaching, sermonizing, or moralizing. He never tried to set up his own standards of right and wrong.

All in all, he was a man's man, and such a man comes along but seldom. I have not seen him for many years now, but I often think of him and the things he stood for. Major McCampbell used miracle people power all the time without even realizing it. With him it had become automatic.

I think you can see from this short description of the Major that after a lot of practice of miracle people power techniques yourself, certain character attributes will grow stronger within you until your miracle people power becomes almost automatic, too. Then you can use it to control, to influence, to guide, and to help others without even thinking about what you're doing.

All these character attributes are really benefits to be gained— not techniques to be employed. For example, if a person is kind, decent, and courteous to others—is that only a technique that he's using? Hardly. It is a benefit, for he'll receive the same kind of treatment in return from his fellow men and women.

I'd like now to cover some of those character attributes for you. A person who keeps his miracle people power at a high level all the time is bound to have most of them. In fact, such an individual—

1. Has a strong belief in human rights and will stand up for the rights of others, even those with whom he disagrees.
2. Has respect for the dignity of every person. Never degrades or attacks the dignity of any individual. Treats every man like a gentleman and every woman like a lady.
3. Uses the Golden Rule attitude toward all his daily associates.
4. Shows an abiding interest in all aspects of human welfare.
5. Exhibits a willingness to deal with every person as considerately as if he were a blood relative.
6. Behaves toward new acquaintances as he does toward old friends and family members.
7. Is not selfish and self-centered. Talks to others in terms of their interests rather than his own.
8. Tolerates and accepts the faults and character defects of those around him. By the same token, does not set up his own standards of right and wrong. Makes allowances for the weaknesses and frailties of others.
9. Keeps a healthy, lively, and active curiosity about everything that will help people.
10. Makes allowances for inexperience.
11. Gives ground on unimportant trifles, but stands fast and firm on principles.
12. Helps everybody whenever, wherever, and however he can.
13. Looks for that within that makes the man, rather than judging by some outside quality.
14. Realizes that what he cannot do does not make a thing impossible to accomplish.
15. Accepts the things that cannot be changed, but has the courage to change the things he can.
16. Does not expect a uniformity of opinions nor does he endeavor to mold all dispositions alike.
17. Does not try to measure the enjoyment of others by his own.
18. Always sets the example for others to follow by being honest, dependable, courageous, and decisive.

19. Exhibits such additional miracle people power traits of character as endurance, enthusiasm, initiative, judgment, justice, loyalty, diplomacy, and tact.

Practice the techniques I've given you and these character attributes will become deeply ingrained in you. The deeper they become and the stronger they grow, the easier it will be to practice the techniques. Your miracle people power will become so automatic you'll be able to keep it at a high level all the time without even half trying.

If nothing else, attainment of the character attributes I've listed in this last chapter will enable you to live with yourself. You'll be able to face yourself in the mirror and sleep comfortably at night without any feeling of self-guilt.

If the ability to live with yourself was the only single benefit to be gained by reading this entire book, as far as I'm concerned, it would be well worthwhile.